THE POWER
TO COMMUNICATE

**Gender Differences
As Barriers**

THE POWER TO COMMUNICATE

Gender Differences As Barriers

Deborah Borisoff
Lisa Merrill

Waveland Press, Inc.
Prospect Heights, Illinois

For information about this book, write or call:

Waveland Press, Inc.
P.O. Box 400
Prospect Heights, Illinois 60070
(312) 634-0081

Artist for Cover Design: Jan De Ruth

Acknowledgement

The authors of this text wish to thank Milton Baxter, Professor of English at the City University of New York for his insightful suggestions and editorial assistance.

ABOUT THE AUTHORS

Deborah Borisoff

Deborah Borisoff, Ph.D., is the Associate Director of the Program in Speech Communication at New York University's School of Education, Health, Nursing, and Arts Professions.

She is on the faculty at New York University, where she has developed and taught courses on *Confrontation Communication, Listening, The Gender Gap, Psychology of Communication,* and *Communication for Professionals.* Several of these courses deal with the ideas presented in this text.

Dr. Borisoff's publications include articles on communication within the professional environment of dentists for *The New York Journal of Dentistry*; hearing in adults for *Vogue*; problems related to hearing in children for *Mother's Manual*; and language development in young children for *Mothers' Today.*

Lisa Merrill

Lisa Merrill, Ph.D., is a writer, drama therapist and communications consultant who is presently teaching Speech and Theatre classes at New York and Hofstra Universities.

She has been on the faculty of Rutgers University and City University of New York. From 1979-1981 Dr. Merrill developed and taught at Douglass College, Rutgers University, *Women as Speakers* focusing on many of the issues in this text.

Dr. Merrill's publications include articles on communicative strategies of women dentists for *The New York Journal of Dentistry*; theatre criticism for *Women and Performance* and cross cultural communication for *Resource.*

Contents

Preface

This book addresses two essential issues that are often missing from works that deal with communication. First, it examines the impact of the stereotyped gender differences that are so powerful a force in male and female development, communication, and in male and female professional contexts.

Second, this book includes strategies and techniques that may be helpful to both women and men in dealing with persistent traditional attitudes and in attempting to break from them.

Following Chapters I, II, III and IV, we have provided numerous activities and exercises that can be used in a variety of instructional and training situations. These activities have been created to target different communication skills such as listening ability, and conflict resolution, and settings, such as one-to-one dyads, small group situations, and public communication contexts.

Introduction

DEFINING THE GENDER GAP
The Need for Cooperation in a Technological Age

Nearly every decade in American culture can be singled out for special achievements or strides. The 1980's is no exception — especially in the area of accomplishments by women. During the initial years of this period, for the first time a woman was appointed to the Supreme Court, served as a member of a space mission, and was nominated as a Vice-Presidential candidate for a major American party. These breakthroughs for women indicate that today America is in the throes of a social revolution in which individuals are expanding upon the traditional expectations for their sex.

While advancements in the area of technology can be clearly measured, social changes are more difficult to assess, often requiring the distance of decades; in some instances, centuries. Within the past two decades, one social issue that has emerged in the forefront of American culture is the gender gap. Because increasing numbers of women are pursuing careers and because many men are sharing more equally the responsibilities of the home, both sexes are now required to demonstrate communicative behavior that previously belonged to the repertoire of the opposite sex. This change in behavior is easier to consider intellectually than it is to achieve because it is no small task to break from our prescribed cultural upbringing. Telling a woman she must be aggressive to succeed in business when she has been raised to be a polite young lady is just as difficult as instructing a man to share equally in the household

1

chores when he was raised by a full-time homemaker who attended to his every need. In both cases, breaking from tradition is required, and this is very hard to do.

Both because the urge to maintain the *status quo* is powerful among many segments of our population, and because many individuals are now striving for opportunities long denied them, it is necessary to understand the consequences of bridging the communication gender gap. To do so, it is necessary to gain an insight into the communicative behavior that is part of the male and female experience in American society. This is exactly what researchers have endeavored to accomplish in recent years.

Research findings have been compiled in a variety of areas that deal with communication differences between the sexes. Physiological and psychological development has been of steady interest and concern to social scientists. Sociological research has increasingly emerged on the role of men and women in society and on their attitudes toward relationships, work, money and sex. The implications of language use as it affects the development and perceived roles of young children in society has been one focus of linguists. And nonverbal behavior as a powerful communication force continues to attract the interest of scholars from a variety of academic disciplines.

The research in the areas of psychology, sociology and linguistics demonstrates that the difference in communication styles between women and men in American culture is very real indeed. Although differences in the behaviors expected of either sex have always existed in our society, the explanations for interpretations of these disparities have changed over time.

For example, a century ago, it was argued that women were ill suited physiologically to intellectual endeavors and that higher education would adversely affect them. At the present time, few would argue that women are biologically unfit for these pursuits. This example demonstrates a shift in perspective supporting the contention that biological factors alone do not determine behavior. Therefore, the distinctions between male and female behavior identified in this text are referred to as gender rather than sex differences because they are socially constructed and not innate.

In this book, we will consider these existing communication differences, implied sexual stereotypes and the barriers these stereotypes impose on men and women. We will also explore successful professional communication strategies and future implications of men and women working more closely together. By examining the differences in communication styles we hope to provide a means to enrich and expand the communication behavior of both men and women. The rewards of such change may accrue not only in the professional arena but also in the area of interpersonal relationships. Both sexes stand to benefit by such an understanding. Both will benefit from a more equal participation in the communication process.

Chapter I

THE STEREOTYPE
Fiction or Fact

"Sir, a woman's preaching is like a dog's walking on his hind legs. It is not done well, but you are surprised to find it done at all."

Samuel Johnson

"Why - do they shut Me out of Heaven
Did I sing - too loud?"

Emily Dickinson

Public speaking is an assertive act. "Speech" and "voice" are frequently used as metaphors for power. It is in the act of giving voice to one's thoughts and feelings that a speaker has the potential to affect the thoughts and behavior of others.

Throughout much of recorded history, women have been forbidden to or actively discouraged from exercising their power of speech in public settings. Female silence has been equated with modesty, obedience, and womanly virtue.[1] Social and religious injunctions against women communicators have abounded. In the *New Testament*, Saint Paul instructed men to "Let a woman learn in silence with all submissiveness." He said, "I permit no woman to teach or to have authority over men; she is to keep silent." (I Timothy 2:9-15).

The authors of this text are both teachers; readers of this text presumably are enlightened twentieth century women and men, yet all of us have been influenced by what historically has been considered *appropriate* communicative behavior for our respective sexes. In this chapter, we discuss the stereotypical expectations placed upon speakers of both sexes, some

5

of the sanctions anticipated and endured by those who violate the 'expectations, and the process by which gender-based stereotypes have been internalized.

I. FEMININE STEREOTYPES

Background

In the 1650's, Anne Hutchinson was exiled from the Massachusetts Bay Colony because she attempted to have a voice in religious affairs. Hutchinson's "crime" was that she led meetings, called "conversations," in her home for groups of sixty or more people who came to listen to her theories about Christ. Her eloquent demeanor infuriated her accusers. John Winthrop, Governor of the Colony, described Hutchinson as "A Woman of a haughty and fierce carriage, of a nimble wit and active spirit and a very voluble tongue."[2] Hutchinson's ease and skill as a communicator were, in part, her crime, as was her usurpation of the male perogative of speaking to an assembled audience. This violated the norms for acceptable womanly behavior. Women were not supposed to be as inherently facile at communicating as men. Consequently, when they spoke in public, they were considered impious or immodest.

In anticipation of a negative reaction, some early women speakers chose to apologize to their audience for the uncharacteristic act. Priscilla Mason said in her Salutatory Oration at the Young Ladies' Academy of Philadelphia on May 15, 1793, "A female, young and inexperienced, addressing a promiscuous assembly is a novelty which requires an apology, as some may suppose. I therefore, with submission beg issue to offer a few thoughts on the vindication of female eloquence."[3] Mason went on to propose that speech, even in public settings, need not be antithetical to current notions of femininity. However, most of Mason's eighteenth and nineteenth century contemporaries vociferously disagreed.

With the coming of industrialization in the nineteenth century, historians affirm that "...role divisions and sexual stereotypes were permanently imprinted in the American popular mind."[4] The vast majority of licensed doctors and educators were male. Most of these men believed, and convinced the populace, that the female brain and internal organs would be injured by sustained intellectual effort. Nevertheless, women reformers, abolitionists and womens' rights activists embarked upon public speaking tours.

Two of the first American women to successfully challenge the notion that public speaking was unfeminine, were abolitionists Sarah and Angelina Grimke. Daughters of a South Carolina slave holding family, the Grimkes moved north to Philadelphia and joined the Quakers, the only large religious denomination in the nineteenth century to allow women to become ordained as ministers. The Grimkes were invited by the American Anti-Slavery Society to speak at what were to be small parlor gatherings of women in New York. At their first meeting, more than three hundred women showed up. On subsequent occasions, men attended as well, and the Grimkes were soon addressing mixed audiences. As with other women who were political activists, people were as much outraged by the audacity of a woman speaking to a mixed audience as offended by anything she might say. In a reaction against the Grimkes, the clergy published a Pastoral Letter from the Massachusetts Council of Congregational Ministers which asserted that, "When woman assumes the place and tone of man as a public reformer...she yields the power which God has given her for protection, and her character becomes unnatural."[5]

Increasingly, throughout the nineteenth century, other American women risked being regarded as "unnatural" as they stood up to speak out on such social and political issues as abolition, temperance, women's right to education and women's right to vote. In fact, the movement for women's rights in the United States was, from the beginning, intimately tied to the struggle by women to speak out on their own behalf.

In 1840, when American abolitionists Lucretia Mott and Elizabeth Cady Stanton met in London at the World Anti-Slavery Convention, they were mortified to find that women were not allowed to participate in the proceedings and were forced to sit passively behind a curtain. These women who had worked so courageously for the abolitionist cause were denied the right to speak at the convention to which they and their spouses had been invited. Out of this outrage, they vowed to organize a convention that would protest against what Stanton called "...the injustice which had brooded for ages over the character and destiny of half the human race."[6] The denial of speech was a paradigm for the other injustices women suffered. Eight years later Stanton and Mott led the Senaca Falls Convention. Most historians cite this event as the origin of the organized women's movement in the United States.

Yet, even on this momentous occasion, the prejudice against women communicators was as strong as the reaction to the speakers' message. Stanton's husband, abolitionist Henry B. Stanton, threatened to leave town if Elizabeth delivered a speech in which she proposed demanding the vote for women. Henry Stanton did leave town, and the long, scholarly, eloquent speech that Elizabeth Cady Stanton delivered was prefaced by an apology. Stanton said to her audience, "I should feel exceedingly diffident to appear before you at this time, having never before spoken in public, were I not nerved by a sense of right and duty...."[7]

Stanton's "diffidence" is understandable when we bear in mind the fact that according to many of her contemporaries, a woman speaking was compromising her modesty, purity and virtue. The women of Stanton's time were expected to "noiselessly" follow their husband's lead.

Nonetheless, there were a few notable exceptions. Stanton's contemporary, activist Lucy Stone, was one of the earliest American women to deliberately prepare herself to undertake a career as a public speaker. After graduating from Oberlin College in 1847, Stone became a professional anti-slavery lecturer. In 1855, when Stone married fellow abolitionist Henry Blackwell, the *Boston Post* published a poem that ended, "A name like Curtius' shall be his/on Fame's loud trumpet blown/ who with a wedding kiss shuts up/ the mouth of Lucy Stone."[8]

Fortunately, the Blackwell-Stone marriage appears to have been a union in which Blackwell supported and encouraged Stone's activism and public speaking. However, implicit in the anonymous verse quoted above is the belief that husbands may "shut up" their wives, and that women who talk too much should be silenced.

Poltical scientist Nannerl O. Keohane has asserted that, "The power of such prescriptive silence is such that when women do speak, their speech sounds strange. It deviates from the norm of masculinity in timbre and in pattern.... And the words of women are consistently devalued in group settings, not heard, assumed to be trivial, not attended to."[9]

Unlike the women activists mentioned above, the *stereotypically feminine speaker is soft spoken, self-effacing, and compliant. More emotional than logical, she is prone to be disorganized and subjective.*

It is obvious that this image of women is biased and restrictive. Let us look in greater detail at these limitations in the feminine stereotype.

Limitations of the Feminine Stereotype.

1. *She is soft spoken.*

Women, like children, have been taught that it is preferable for them to be seen rather than to be heard. When heard, female voices are apt to be considered abrasive or displeasing, and their words devoid of serious meaning.

If we examine some of the more pejorative adjectives that can be used to describe speakers, we see that in addition to Hutchinson's "voluble" tongue, a voice may be considered carping, brassy, nagging, shrill, strident or grating. Conversing may be referred to as babbling, blabbing, gabbing or chattering. Although these terms are not specifically gender identified, they are commonly used to describe the speech behavior of females and each implies the superficial or trivial nature of the speaker's message. Women have internalized this socially imposed stereotype and in many cases, have brought with them into any public setting a deeply rooted reticence to speaking out.

Sociologist Lucille Duberman has explained that "To internalize means...to adopt the standards of one's society as part of one's self image, so that the attitudes and behaviors approved by the society appear to have no possible alternatives."[10] By accepting and internalizing the stereotypical view of women as communicators, women are discouraged from using their voice to assert a point strongly. The soft-spoken woman's voice does not carry. She threatens no one, but she may lack sufficient force and volume to speak up effectively and convincingly. Women who are hampered by the need to sound feminine may adopt a high-pitched "little girl" voice, an artificially "sexy" breathy voice, or a volume so low as to be barely audible. In any case, the "soft spoken" woman is at a marked disadvantage if she attempts to negotiate a contract, persuade a jury, or present a report.

2. *She is self-effacing.*

To some extent, women's messages are ignored, interrupted and not attended to because women are taught, according to Robin Lakoff, to "talk like a lady," to use disclaimers, (e.g., "This may not be right, but...."), weak particles, (e.g., "Dear me," "Goodness," etc.), tag questions, (e.g., "The book was good, wasn't it?"), and to reflect uncertainty.[11] When women do not employ these tactics, they may be accused of being unfeminine; but if they do "talk like a lady," they risk not being taken seriously. Consequently, the stereotype of the female speaker as insecure, superficial, and weak becomes self-perpetuating. Having been historically discouraged from speaking, women internalize the stereotype and fear violating the norm. This fear leads to the acculturated adoption of communicative strategies that are hyper-polite, constructed to please by minimizing one's own skills rather than to risk antagonizing one's audience. These are the tactics of less powerful individuals, and when women adopt them, which they overwhelmingly do regardless of socio-economic stature, the perception of women's relative weakness as communicators is confirmed.

3. *She is compliant.*

The diffidence or insecurity experienced by the speaker who is conscious of her violation of societal norms may be manifested in several ways. Rather than be labeled "unnatural" or "unfeminine," a woman may engage in what Janet Stone and Jane Bachner have called "self-trivializing messages" that register the speaker's insecurity, doubt and eagerness to please.[12]

The compliant speaker allows herself to be interrupted. She moves out of the way when someone approaches her. She smiles often to assure the good will of others. She maintains eye contact and listens attentively while others speak, but averts her eyes when she is the focus of attention. The compliant woman demonstrates her submissiveness through these communicative behaviors, which are characteristics of subordinates in a hierarchy. Those who are perceived as, and who perceive themselves as less powerful, tend to employ verbal and nonverbal tactics calculated to appease rather than to threaten their listeners. Women who do not engage in these behaviors have often been criticized by the public.

4. *She is emotional and subjective.*

This aspect of the feminine stereotype directly affects the female speaker's credibility. A speaker is considered credible when she or he can demonstrate competence, dynamism, consistency and co-orientation with an audience. The more subjective a speaker appears, the less likely she or he will be able to support a point with evidence from other acknowledged sources. Audiences regard as less credible a message built on feelings rather than on facts. Yet mathematician Evelyn Fox Keller has called into question "the mythology that casts objectivity, reason and mind as male, and subjectivity, feeling and nature as female."[13] Keller suggests that we see through the myth of objectivity in order to examine "the influence of our own desires, wishes and beliefs" on the claims and discoveries we make."[14]

Nonetheless, we have been conditioned to view objectivity as superior to subjectivity. This is part of the lens through which women and men have been taught to view the world. Simone de Beauvoir wrote that "Representation of the world, like the world itself, is the work of men. They describe it from their own point of view, which they confuse with the absolute truth."[15] It is from this "truth" that our masculine and feminine stereotypes have evolved.

II. MASCULINE STEREOTYPES

Background

Rhetoric is one of the oldest academic disciplines. Originating in the Western world with the Greeks, the formal study of oral discourse as a means of persuasion and of finding "truth," was based upon masculine communication models. Walter J. Ong wrote that, "Rhetoric developed in the past as a major ex-

pression of the rational level of ceremonial combat which is
found among males and typically only among males at the physical level throughout the entire animal kingdom."[16] Ong claimed
that not only was the masculine model of communication based
on confrontation and conflict, but that, as a result, academic
education, which was for centuries the exclusive province of
males until the romantic age, was based on "defending a position (thesis) or attacking the position of another person."[17] All
disciplines were taught by this method.

In western societies, men have been reared to confront, to
compete, to challenge and to win; women have been taught to
acquiesce, to accommodate and to compromise. When placed
within the framework of communication, this gender-linked behavior leads males to gravitate towards delivering organized
public speeches and debates, while women are encouraged to
mediate and to listen. In most cultures, implicit in this division
of tasks is a hierarchy of values.

Historically, men have had almost exclusive access to formal
language training and to education. In the Judeo-Christian tradition, men learned and spoke Hebrew and Latin. One of the
dicta of Rabbinic Judaism was, "cursed be the man who
teaches his daughter Torah."[18] In religion, politics and education men were afforded the right and given the encouragement
to learn, to speak what they knew, and to use their speech to
effectuate their desires.

Males have been taught to be logical, objective and impersonal; while women have been encouraged to be subjective,
self-disclosing and personal. Always, however, the "masculine" traits have been afforded greater status. Women render themselves vulnerable by their self-disclosure; men derive
power from sounding authoritative and communicating facts
rather than emotions.

Many communication texts employ metaphors for aggression
in their discussion of rhetoric. Speakers are instructed to
"arm" themselves against the other speaker's "argument"; to
"win" their point by "waging an attack" on the "weak" points
in their "opponents" logic with a strong "plan of battle." This
is a specifically male formula based on ancient Greek philo-
sophers, statesmen and orators.

This tradition demonstrates how a male stereotype has developed throughout history. *The masculine model is that of a speaker who is direct, confrontative, forceful and logical; whose few, well-chosen words are focused on making a particular point.*

There are two major drawbacks to this model. First, unlike the specifically "feminine" stereotypes, the male version appears to be neutral rather than gender specific. Simone de Beauvoir has explained that masculine values and behavior have been considered the desirable "human" norm, while feminine values and behavior have been regarded as aberrant and "other."[19] It is, therefore, often difficult for men to see that the male generic is, in fact, the "male-specific." Consequently, men have resisted identifying the limitations of their role and expanding upon it. The limitations in the "feminine" stereotype as we have identified it are explicit. However, we need to dig deeper to uncover the negative implications in the male role.

Limitations of the Male Stereotype

1. *He is an ineffective listener.*

One deficiency in the male stereotype has been the negative association for listening. As we have established, speaking is active, but, often, listening has been portrayed as passive, weak, or "feminine" behavior. Because much of their survival has depended upon the ability to read and decode accurately the verbal and nonverbal clues of their superiors, women, (and all subordinates in hierarchies), have developed their listening skills more effectively. Gloria Steinem has claimed that women's so-called "intuition" is a manifestation of their better developed listening skills.[20]

When a man has been reared to regard his own message as paramount, all too often he interrupts other speakers and/or takes time while others are speaking, to prepare his own response mentally, rather than to attend to the messages of others. According to researchers Don H. Zimmerman and Candace West, in mixed-sex pairs, men overwhelmingly interrupt women.[21]

2. *He may not express his emotions.*

Another communication weakness that Warren Farrell ironically lists among the "Ten Commandments of Masculinity" is the dictum that because men "shalt not be vulnerable," they may not express fear, weakness, sympathy, empathy or involvement.[22] Because they are taught to value the logical, practical and intellectual to the exclusion of the emotional, males find it difficult to communicate emotions (except anger). When one partner is routinely more self-disclosing and, therefore, more vulnerable, the result is a hierarchical rather than an egalitarian relationship. Thus, in situations when men most desire intimacy and trust, the masculine dictum against expressing emotions may prove an enormous impediment.

3. *He makes categorical assertions.*

The masculine stereotype encourages men to be authoritative and to make sweeping claims. This behavior appears to reflect self-assurance. However, by avoiding the feminine communicative mode of qualification and indirection, men may in fact be limited by their assertions. Carol Gilligan asserts that the tendency of women to *be* more indirect and open to options can be an asset, not only a form of deference born of women's social subordination. As Gilligan states, "Sensitivity to the needs of others and the assumption of the responsibility for taking care lead women to attend to voices other than their own and to include in their judgement other points of view."[23] When individuals sincerely desire open and honest communication among equals, they need to resist categorical assertions that reflect a preconceived mind set.

4. *He dominates the discussion.*

A final aspect of the masculine stereotype is the assumption that men speak significantly less than women. In the other gender-linked communication traits mentioned earlier, research has borne out the fact that female and male behavior does not generally reflect the respective stereotypes. However, numerous studies have shown that the assumption that men are less talkative than women is based on fiction rather than on fact.[24] In mixed-sex groups, men routinely speak more than women, and, in fact, usually dominate the conversations. Men are more likely to introduce the topics to be discussed, to interrupt others, and to initiate the changing of topics. Much of women's talk is devoted to drawing men into conversation, and offering a number of topics from which males may choose.

Furthermore, when male silence occurs in mixed-sex discussions, it does not necessarily denote listening. The withholding of speech also can imply power. Superiors need not answer subordinates, but subordinates are usually compelled to respond to superiors. However, equal "veto" power in a conversation is necessary for individuals to feel that they have established an effective communication climate. Therefore, any individual who dominates a discussion, negatively influences the communication climate.

III. NONVERBAL ASPECTS OF THE STEREOTYPES

The feminine and masculine stereotypes that we have identified thus far have nonverbal components as well. As with verbal gender-linked traits, the nonverbal distinctions also imply a power differential. Psychologist Nancy Henley has identified gestures that communicate dominance and submission in this culture.

Dominance	Submission
Stare	Lower eyes, avert gaze, blink
Touch	Cuddle to the touch
Interrupt	Stop talking
Crowd another's space	Yield, move away
Frown, look stern	Smile
Point	Move in pointed direction; obey[25]

We can observe that gestures of dominance are stereotypically male, and those of submission are stereotypically female. When power differences are communicated nonverbally, they are extremely difficult to isolate and to identify in context. As a result, much of how we picture gender differences appears innate rather than as a function of a pervasive, learned nonverbal communication behavior pattern.

In Chapters I and II, we will examine specific ways that masculinity and femininity are communicated nonverbally. At this point, however, it is important to note that cultural stereotypes for men and women, whether communicated through verbal or nonverbal channels, are as much symbols of power or powerlessness as they are models of gender differences.

In this chapter we have identified three important stereotypes: that of the "naturally" insecure, superficial and weak
woman, and the "unnaturally" talkative, loud and abrasive
one. Both of these images are limiting. We have explored the
negative implications of the masculine model of a "confrontative" "logical" man of few words. For the most part, these
stereotypes represent actual traits that women and men have
been reared to display. To that extent, they may be considered
social "fact." But since gender-linked traits are learned,
rather than innate behaviors, the stereotypes are also a
"fiction."

The models of femininity and masculinity that we have internalized have been with us for centuries. Throughout history,
women and men have been penalized for violating societal
norms. Women have been called "unnatural" and masculine;
men, "effeminate." Now, at the close of the twentieth century,
it has become apparent that a rigid adherence to the sex role
stereotypes is a disadvantage. We believe that individuals are
capable of creating other, less limiting, more androgynous communication models. But in order to accomplish this, we first
must examine in greater detail the specific verbal and
nonverbal behaviors through which our respective stereotypes
are manifested.

SUGGESTED ACTIVITIES

A. Focus on Listening: Vocal Stereotyping.

Listen to a television soap opera with which you are unfamil-
iar. Turn off the picture and only listen to the voices. See if you
can identify the "good," "bad," "sexy," "intelligent," and
"dumb" character types by their vocal qualities.

a) What are vocal characteristics of the "good" young wife?
The debutante? The manipulator? What about the tough guy?
The sincere, young lover?

b) How is socio-economic class indicated vocally?

c) Do the characters' voices remind you of anyone you know?
If so, do you have similar associations for both the character
and your acquaintance because of how she or he sounds?

B. Focus on Interpersonal/Dyadic Communication and Vocal Stereotyping.

1. Keep track of individuals to whom you speak who have noticeably different speech patterns than your own. Try to use their intonation pattern and mode of articulation when you converse. Note what happens.

a) Is your partner aware of your adjustment?

b) Does she or he think you sound "natural"?

c) Is your partner more open and self-disclosing when you sound alike?

2. Tape a conversation between yourself and a speaker with a different native language. Listen to the pitch and intonation patterns, and note the differences.

a) What attitudes or character traits would these vocal behaviors connote for native American English speakers?

b) Have you assumed that your partner is shy, argumentative, elusive, or confrontative on the basis of an ethnocentric evaluation of vocal traits?

Footnotes

[1] Nannerl O. Keohane, "Speaking from Silence: Women and the Science of Politics," in A Feminist Perspective in the Academy, ed. Elizabeth Langland and Walter Gove (Chicago: University of Chicago Press, 1981), p. 91.

[2] Antinominianism in the Colony of Massachusetts Bay 1636-1638, 21 (Boston: Prince Society Publications, 1894), 158.

[3] As quoted in The Rise and Progress of the Young Ladies' Academy of Philadelphia, (Philadelphia: Steward and Cochran, 1794), p. 95. Also cited in Ann Gordon, "The Young Ladies' Academy of Philadelphia," in Women of America: A History, ed. Carol Ruth Berkin and Mary Beth Norton, (Boston: Houghton Mifflin Co., 1979), pp. 89-90.

[4] Mary P. Ryan, Womanhood in America, (New York: Franklin Watts, 1975), p. 75.

[5] "Pastoral Letter of the General Association of Massachusetts to the Churches Under their Care," The Liberator (Boston), 11 Aug., 1837).

[6] Wendy Martin, American Sisterhood: Writings of the Feminist Movement from Colonial Times to the Present, (New York: Harper and Row, Publishers, Inc., 1972), p. 42.

[7] As quoted in Eleanor Flexner, Century of Struggle; the Woman's Rights Movement in the United States, (New York: Atheneum, 1968), pp. 76-77.

[8] Ibid., p. 70.

[9] Keohane, pp. 91-92.

[10]Lucille Duberman, *Gender and Sex in Society*, (New York: Praeger Publishers, Inc., 1975), p. 27.

[11]Robin Lakoff, *Language and Woman's Place*, (New York: Harper and Row Publishers, 1975), p. 54.

[12]Janet Stone and Jane Bachner, *Speaking Up: A Book for Every Woman who Wants to Speak Effectively*, (New York: McGraw Hill Book Co., 1977), p. 10.

[13]Evelyn Fox Keller, "Feminism as an Analytic Tool for the Study of Science," *Academe*, (Bulletin of the American Association of University Professors), September-October 1983, p. 15.

[14]Ibid., p. 16.

[15]Simone de Beauvoir, *The Second Sex*, trans., and ed. by H.J. Parshley, (New York: Bantam Books, Alfred A. Knopf, Inc., 1952), p. 133.

[16]Walter Ong, "Review of Brian Vickes' *Classical Rhetoric in English Poetry*," *College English*, February 1972 as quoted in Adrienne Rich, *On Lies Secrets and Silence: Selected Prose 1966-1978*, (New York: W.W. Norton & Co., Inc., 1979), p. 128.

[17]Ibid.

[18]Rosemary Radford Ruether, "The Feminist Critique in Religious Studies," Langland and Grove, p. 52.

[19]Simone de Beauvoir, p. XVI ff.

[20]Gloria Steinem, "Men and Women Talking," in *Outrageous Acts and Everyday Rebellions*, (New York: Holt, Rinehart, Winston, 1983), p. 180.

[21]Don H. Zimmerman and Candace West, "Sex Roles, Interruptions and Silences in Conversation," in Barrie Thorne and Nancy Henley, eds., *Language and Sex: Differences and Dominance*, (Rowley, Mass.: Newbury House, 1975), pp. 105-125.

[22]Warren Farrell, "Beyond Masculinity: Liberating Men and their Relationships with Women," in Duberman, p. 224.

[23]Carol Gilligan, *In a Different Voice: Psychological Theory and Women's Development*, (Cambridge, Mass.: Harvard University Press, 1982), p. 16.

[24]Michael Argyle, Mansur Lalljee and Mark Cook, "The Effects of Visibility on Interaction in a Dyad," *Human Relations*, 21 (1968), 3-17, and Fred L. Strodtbeck and Richard D. Mann, "Sex Role Differentiation in Jury Deliberations," *Sociometry*, 19 (1956), 3-11.

[25]Nancy Henley, *Body Politics: Power, Sex and Non Verbal Communication*, (Englewood Cliffs, N.J.: Prentice Hall, 1977), p. 187.

Chapter II

VOCAL, VERBAL AND NONVERBAL BEHAVIOR

> [Woman] must have the skill to incline us to do everything which her sex will not enable her to do for herself...she should also have the art, by her own conversation, actions, looks and gestures, to communicate those sentiments which are agreeable to (men), without seeming to intend it.
>
> Jean Jacques Rousseau
> *Emilius*

Women and men use language differently. How we sound, what words we use and how we order those words all differ in male and female English usage.

Let us begin with how we sound. Fully as much as how we look, how we sound ultimately influences the way people react to us. People make assumptions and form judgements about each other on the basis of speech. Group solidarity is formed and reinforced by commonalities in articulation and pronunciation.

I. VOCAL BEHAVIORS

A. Articulation; or "How correct do you sound?"

Articulation comes from the Latin word for joint. It refers to the joining together of the organs of articulation (e.g., lips, tongue, teeth, glottis, etc.) so as to chop the breath stream into individual sounds. All speakers do not produce and pronounce speech sounds in the same way. For example, if one neglects to place his or her tongue tip between the upper and lower teeth in an attempt to produce a "th" sound (θ or $\eth$), the result may sound like "t" or "d" as in the case of the speaker who says "dese tree tings" for "these three things."

Women are largely judged by their appearance, and speech strongly affects how they appear to others. Numerous studies have established that women are more likely to use standard phonetic grammatical forms than men. Males of similar socioeconomic groups employ more casual and colloquial speech than females. Roger Shuy's study of seven hundred Detroit residents demonstrated that males were more likely to nasalize the (æ) vowel and drop "ing" endings in favor of the more casual "in'."[1] For example: "The man was walkin' and talkin.'" William Labov's studies in New York and Chicago,[2] Peter Trudgill's research on British speakers in Norwich, England[3] and Walter Wolfram's studies of Black speakers in Detroit[4] all indicate that women in each respective group use more standard forms.

Trudgill offers two explanations for this phenomenon. He believes that because women within each social strata are subordinate to men, they must "secure and signal their status linguistically...."[5] Second, since less formal, more working-class pronunciation is associated with toughness and masculinity, women are encouraged to talk like "ladies."

Having taught and lived in working-class environments, it has been our experience that many males have been raised to believe that studying and improving one's articulation is an effeminate undertaking. They seem to fear that attention to standard grammar and articulation will cause others to consider them less masculine. Yet the ability to employ standard articulatory and grammatical forms is of considerable importance for males as well as for females. Because standard forms are equated with higher socioeconomic status, males who resist adopting standard speech in professional or public settings may find their career options impeded. When applying for a job, fighting a traffic ticket, looking for an apartment, dealing with any forms of authority, the ability to assume standard speech can be considered an asset.

B. Pitch: or "How big do you sound?"

A fundamental difference in the way that women and men sound is that women's voices are generally higher pitched than men's. It is partially the size of one's vocal tract that determines pitch. Over the past several years, numerous female students who have registered for our Women as Speakers and Gender Gap classes, bemoaned the fact that nature had saddled them with squeaky, high-pitched, "little girl" voices. However, studies by Ignatius Mattingly[6] in 1966, and Jacqueline Sachs, Philip Lieberman and Donna Erickson[7] in 1973 indicate that the differences in male and female pitch are much greater than anatomical variations logically could explain. Mattingly studied three classes of speakers: men, women and children. He found that male and female speakers of the same dialect tend to form vowels differently thereby affecting the pitch. Mattingly concluded this was a social and linguistic convention. Sachs, *et al.* studied preadolescent children with larynxes of the same size relative to their weight. Adult judges were able to identify the sex of the children solely by listening to tapes of their voices. Sachs, Lieberman and Erickson have hypothesized that, regardless of the size of the larynx and vocal cords, males and females may be adjusting their pitch to fit cultural expectations and stereotypes.

A large person would be expected to have longer, thicker vocal cords and therefore would speak with a lower pitch. A small person with shorter, thinner vocal cords would be expected to have a higher pitched voice. However, individuals may change their pitch by changing the position of their lips when producing vowel sounds. More open lips shorten the vocal tract and thus raise the pitch. For example, women who speak while smiling produce higher pitched sounds than those who do not. Although Sachs *et al.* do not discount the fact that hormonal differences may account for some variation, they speculate that by adjusting the way sounds are produced *males tend to make themselves sound as though they are larger and females as though they are smaller than the articulatory mechanism alone would suggest.* (Later in this chapter we will discuss the extent to which size communicates power nonverbally.) Thus, by adopting excessively high-pitched voices, women are limiting themselves. Women who have assumed this vocal type sound giddy and childish, and they are frequently not taken seriously. The high-pitched childish voice not only diminishes them in size, it diminishes their credibility.

For many years women were denied access to careers in broadcasting on the pretext that the higher-pitched female voice did not sound serious enough, although in France the female voice has been *preferred* for news broadcasting. Here in the United States, we have grown considerably from the time when the only female voices on the nightly news were those of the "cute" (i.e., not serious) "weather girls." Interestingly enough, when broadcast weather predictions became more scientific, the weather girl was replaced by a male meteorologist. However, we still tend to regard the lower-pitched male voice as the voice of authority. Overwhelmingly, male voices are used in commercial voiceovers, even for household products that are purchased and used almost exclusively by women.

Lower-pitched voices seem to be regarded more positively in both women and men. Women's voices that are used in the broadcast media tend to be lower-pitched than those of the female population at large. In fact, William Austin found that the act of *imitating a person of either sex* with a derogatory, high-pitched feminine voice was perceived as an infuriating "act of aggression."[8] Since an artificially high pitch connotes timidity, childishness and/or weakness, it is not surprising that most individuals would be insulted to be depicted in this fashion. What then, are the implications for women whose natural voices are somewhat higher than those of men?

First, women need to be aware of whether they are in effect diminishing themselves by employing a higher pitch than necessary. If so, they must examine the settings in which they are most likely to use their "little girl" voice. Does this occur most frequently with friends, lovers, parents, or employers? Is it a subconscious strategy women adopt when they fear that their message might threaten the person with whom they speak? It may be that women adopt this guise of powerlessness when they anticipate resentment of their strength.

Second, speakers can practice exercises to lower their pitch. (See suggested activities at the end of the chapter). And third, all of us need to guard against judging individuals as if their pitch were a barometer of their capabilities, intelligence or maturity.

C. Intonation; or "How certain to you sound?"

Related to pitch is the more specific area of intonation or inflection. While pitch refers to the general high or low quality of the voice, intonation refers to the pitch swings or changes within a phrase or sentence. Every language has its own intonation patterns. American English speakers usually employ a rising intonation for most questions (except those preceded by interrogative words, e.g.: *who, what, when, where, why,* and *how*), to express hesitancy or uncertainty, and to indicate incompleteness of a thought (as in listing items in a series). A falling intonation is used to give commands, state facts, and to ask questions.

However, Ruth Brend has found that certain intonation patterns are used almost exclusively by women, and are consistently avoided by men.[9] According to Brand's research, females tend to use upward inflections that serve to request confirmation from listeners. Men tend to avoid final patterns that do not end at the lowest pitch level. For example, the female professional is much more likely to invite someone in to her office with an upward inflected "come in." Her male counterpart's "come in" with a downward glide may sound more like a command than a polite request.

Robin Lakoff also identified the hesitation and uncertainty that are implied by women's traditional intonation patterns.[10] Lakoff found that when offering a declarative answer to a question, women often use a rising pattern, which sounds as though they were asking for confirmation or approval, or doubting their own answer. For example, in response to the question, "When are you free to meet with me?" the female speaker may reply "In about...twenty minutes...?" Had she replied "In twenty minutes." with a downward pattern, her message would imply that the addressee had no choice but to wait. This intonation pattern would support a superior, rather than a subordinate position. However, the stereotypically feminine rising pitch pattern sounds more polite in that it *appears* as if the speaker is leaving the decision open rather than imposing her decision upon the addressee.

We must become cognizant of the extent to which vocal behavior is interpreted as a signal of the speaker's attitude about him- or herself and toward the listener. We need also be aware that in different languages and dialects, pitch, intonation patterns and degree of precision in articulation carry different connotations. The English as a Second Language instructor who encourages opposite sex foreign students merely to imitate her or his pitch and intonation patterns without understanding the social connotations of these patterns may be compounding rather than alleviating their problems. In our attitudes about men and women, and native speakers of other languages, we need to be careful not to confuse how we sound with what we mean to say.

II. VERBAL CONSTRUCTS

A. Tag Questions; or "This is what I meant, isn't it?"

When the unarticulated message of hesitancy or doubt implicit in women's rising intonation is expressed in words, the result may take the form known as a tag question. Robin Lakoff has defined a tag question as "midway between an outright statement and a yes/no question."[11] An example of a tag question is, "We have an appointment at three o'clock, don't we?" The tag, "don't we?" represents an attempt to gain confirmation or approval from one's listener. This speaker is avoiding committing her- or himself to an outright statement, while trying to hedge against one of the possible responses of a bipolar (yes-no) question. If the speaker asks, "Do we have an appointment at three o'clock?", she risks receiving a negative or affirmative answer. The tag question is also, therefore, a form of leading question in that the respondent is led in a particular direction.

1. Legitimate Uses of Tag Questions

Lakoff believes that there are some occasions when a tag question is "legitimate." When an individual has only partial information, she/he may ask a tag question for confirmation. For example, "You have been teaching for ten years, haven't you?"

Tag questions are also used frequently in small talk as a way to initiate a conversation, as in "The bus is very late, isn't it?"

2. *Inappropriate Uses of Tag Questions*

When tag questions are used when discussing opinions, often the listener is left with an impression of the speaker's uncertainty. A person who says, "This is well written, isn't it?" may be resisting the assertion of her or his own opinion. The agreement or disagreement of the addressee is given weight over the speaker's judgement. In such instances, the speaker then sounds uncertain and insecure.

Tag questions are also inappropriate when they are intentionally manipulative. Depending upon the intonation used, it may be condescending to ask, "You *will* have the report finished on time, won't you?" The addressee in this case is being led towards the particular response preferable to the speaker. If the speaker wanted an honest answer s/he could inquire, "Will you have the report ready on time?" However, the tag form is still more polite than the command, "Have the report ready on time."

Speakers need to become aware of their reasons for electing to use tag questions. Although the tag form is indirect, it is not inherently weak or strong. The tag question may be quite effective as a means of drawing listeners into a conversation. By asking a question in this form, a speaker may be telling a listener that his or her perceptions or opinions are being given consideration.

However, at times it is ineffective for speakers to cloak their personal opinions in tag forms since such usage reflects uncertainty about their own opinions. Individuals who are seen as, and who regard themselves as powerless need others to validate their opinions. Lakoff believes that more women than men use tag questions precisely in this manner.

B. Qualifiers; or "I sort of think maybe you know what I mean."

The use of qualifiers (such as *maybe, probably, rather, kind of, sort of, really, I think,* and *I guess*) is also more common in the speech of women than in men. These expressions dilute statements by indicating the speaker's lack of confidence. The surgeon who says, "I kind of think you need an operation" will not be regarded as someone with whose judgement one may feel confident.

A qualifier softens the statements in which it appears. "I am sort of disappointed in your work this quarter" sounds less devastating to a listener than the unqualified statement. Even the words "actually" and "really" which may appear at first glance to strengthen an expression, do in fact soften it. "I *really* don't want to be disturbed" is less assertive than affirming "I *don't* want to be disturbed." The need for "really" and "actually" may imply that the speaker believes that she or he will not be taken seriously without the added emphasis.

We need to listen carefully to our own voices and become accustomed to excising unnecessary qualifiers from our speech. When we qualify statements, they sound less categorical, less permanent, and thus, safer. Qualified statements are less likely to offend listeners. However, if they are employed routinely, whenever one needs to make a verbal stand, these "crutches" may get in the way. A police officer, for example, who advises a suspect, "I think maybe you should call your lawyer" may not be perceived as a strong authority figure.

C. Vocabulary differences; or "Which words are whose?"

Certain words and categories of words appear much more frequently in women's speech than in men's. Adverbs of intensity (such as *awfully, terribly, pretty, quite, so,* and the adjectives *charming, lovely, adorable, divine, cute* and *sweet*) are more common in women's usage.

Women also have a much more extensive vocabulary for colors than men. Words for colors like *taupe, beige, mauve, lavender* and *violet* are not common in men's speech. Males are not expected to discuss the "lovely mauve drapes" in the conference room, or the "streaks of lavender" in the sunset. When men do use words that are stereotypically part of the female lexicon, they risk being considered effeminate.

Some theorists believe that words women use lead listeners to regard them as trivial and superficial because of the attention paid to subtle distinctions and details — such as color gradations. However, we could argue that the ability to discern and to describe more subtle differences in color is a strength in women's speech; not a detriment. Nonetheless, it is important for female speakers to note that their message is likely to be regarded as superficial and irrelevant when they use such phrases as "the taupe attache case" for example. The problem does not lie in the words, but in the *connotation* these words have for the listeners who hear them.

Men are afforded the right to use specific words that, until recently, were rarely present in women's speech. Forceful expletives like *damn*, and *hell* are considered much more acceptable in men's speech than in women's. Women risk being considered unfeminine when they use these words. Instead, women have been encouraged to be polite, and to use such expressions as *dear me, oh my,* and *goodness.* These particles are less forceful than those allowed men, and their use tends to weaken or to render trivial the expression which follows. For example, it would sound ludicrous for the female executive to say, "Dear me, you mean we lost the multimillion dollar contract?", or the female attorney to remark, "Oh, goodness. I hope we don't have another hung jury."

Increasingly women in all fields are more likely to employ the expletives found in male speech to convey strong emotions while men rarely, if ever, use "women's" particles. Men are likely to be stigmatized for their use of feminine words. As Lakoff explains, "The language of the favored group, the group that holds power....is generally adopted by the other group, and not vice versa."[12]

D. Disclaimers; or "This probably doesn't mean anything, but..."

The use of disclaimers is an obvious sign to listeners that a speaker is not, or does not consider him- or herself to be a member of the dominant group. Females often preface their remarks with disclaimers like "This probably isn't important, but...", or "I'm really not sure about this, however..."

By using these expressions, the speaker attempts to distance her- or himself from the claim, rather than to stand behind it. The disclaimer serves in part as an apology for speaking, and also in part, as a plea to an audience not to associate the speaker too closely with the message. This protective device assures the speaker that the message may be rejected without the *speaker* being rejected.

When individuals use disclaimers, their message is weakened *before* it is uttered, since it appears as though they are not knowledgeable or prepared or lack strong conviction. Disclaimers are found more frequently in women's speech than in men's. They also are found often in the speech of non-native English speakers. Disclaimers manifest the speaker's perception that one has to apologize in advance to gain the good will of an audience that would otherwise not be receptive.

In our work with female students and with non-native English speakers, we have encouraged students to eliminate disclaimers from their speech. The use of a disclaimer may be a strategy to ingratiate oneself to a possibly prejudiced or inattentive audience. However, in addition to speakers being advised to avoid such strategies, listeners also need to be aware that their responses to speakers may be encouraging the use of disclaimers. Listeners bear a responsibility to demonstrate verbally and nonverbally that they are receptive to the speaker.

When women and nonnative English speakers are made to feel that they are being listened to willingly and with concentration, they will be less likely to punctuate their remarks with disclaimers. While we encourage women to abandon the self-effacing strategy, we recommend that listeners ask themselves, "What have I done or am I doing to make this speaker feel that she or he is not worthy of my attention?"

E. Compound Requests; or "How many words shall I use to make my wishes known?"

Despite stereotypes to the contrary, women often have more difficulty voicing requests and demands than men. Individuals who are accustomed to wielding considerable personal power are more likely to use imperatives than are subordinates. For example, "Type this now!" is a command issued by a speaker who assumes that his or her authority is such that the addressee is compelled to comply. On the other hand, "Please type this now" and "Will you type this now?" are both requests. The addressee is being asked to go along with the speaker, but may refuse.

Lakoff maintains that women tend to compound their requests by asking either "Will/Can you please type this now?"

or "Won't you please type this now?" The more a request is compounded, the more polite it sounds, because the listener has increasingly greater latitude to refuse the request. The most indirect request, "If it's not too much trouble, won't you please type this now?" is worded negatively to imply the greater possibility of the addressee's refusal.

Speakers and listeners of both sexes should be aware of how they choose to phrase their requests. Those who routinely employ indirect compound forms may find that, on occasion, a more direct, less apologetic tone is more expedient. However, speakers who characteristically use imperatives need to take responsibility for *how* they phrase their messages as well as for what they say. Many male speakers, in particular, are baffled when their listeners bridle against being *ordered* to do something that the speaker *intended* as a *request* rather than as a command. Both strategies—direct and polite—are necessary skills to master.

Men and women have been taught to use language differently. For women, speech communication is a social medium. Women have been raised to use communication as a mechanism for creating bonds. Men have been encouraged to communicate primarily to exchange information. Tag questions, qualifiers, disclaimers, and intonation patterns that sound as though the speaker is requesting rather than commanding, are strategies common to women's speech. These verbal and vocal behaviors are considered less direct, but more polite than the corresponding patterns males tend to employ. And yet, lest these be presented as two equal options, it must be remembered that *the need to be polite* is in itself a signal of a power imbalance. Subordinates who fear alienating their superiors are required to be polite. Politeness is a strategy for gaining or maintaining favor. Those already powerful are not compelled to be polite. They can therefore afford to be direct.

In this text, we do not propose one absolute model of directedness or politeness for speakers of both sexes, nor do we wish to reinforce sex role stratified differences in speech. We see neither model as inherently weak or strong. Rather, we would hope that all individuals might increase their repertoire of strategies and responses.

III. VERBAL AND VOCAL DIFFERENCES IN CONTEXT

Thus far we have been examining vocal and verbal gender differences as they relate to individual speakers. But speaking is a dynamic exchange between two or more people. Having established in what ways women and men speak differently, we will now explore what happens when they speak with each other.

Interruptions, Fillers, and Control of Topic

Dyadic communication refers to communication between two individuals. Men and women are engaged in mixed sex dyads as friends, lovers, spouses, colleagues, employers and employees, clinicians and patients, teachers and students, etc. (In Chapter III we discuss the specific applications of dyadic communication in the professional setting.)

One person speaks; another listens, comments on what she or he has heard, and offers a message which is, in turn, heard and responded to by the first speaker. A simple conversation? Perhaps. However, when the members of the dyad are opposite sexes, often a hierarchy of power is established and maintained.

Whether in the job interview or at the dinner table, men tend to interrupt women more often, and seize control of the topic discussed. Women allow themselves to be interrupted, and are more likely to use fillers like "mmm hmm," "well," and "you know."

As Don Zimmerman and Candace West found in their study (cited in Chapter I), virtually all the interruptions and overlaps (cases in which two individuals speak at the same time) they witnessed were initiated by men.[13] Fred Strodtbeck, in his studies on jury deliberation, found that men and persons of higher status spoke more than women and persons of lower status.[14] Speech, as we have established, indicates power. In many dyads, women have a hard time getting the floor.

When women in mixed sex pairs, or in small groups with men, do have the opportunity to be heard, usually it is when they are discussing a topic of the man's choosing. Zimmerman and West found that when women try to introduce topics, they often meet minimal responses from males. On the other hand, when men speak, women tend to be overeager to provide support. Female listeners use fillers like "I see," "Really?" and "mmm hmm," which encourage the speaker to continue.

In the work setting, these gender-linked behaviors may present enormous difficulties. From the first job interview, women and men need to be particularly cognizant of the impact of gender expectations on their respective communication strategies. All too often, in a job interview, the interviewee perceives of her- or himself as a passive participant subject to the interviewer's whims. However, to be successful, interviewees need to be active, well prepared, and able to shift and refocus questions. If the hierarchy of the job interview is further compounded by tendencies of a male interviewer to interrupt and to dominate verbally a female applicant, it will be an unsuccessful experience for both participants. The same potential conflicts exist in exchanges between loan officers and applicants, doctors and patients and teachers and students. In fact, all dyadic interactions in which members of the dyad have differing degrees of power and status are further polarized when the individuals are opposite sexes.

As a way of diminishing the power differential between men and women, we suggest the following strategies.

1. In every interruption or overlap, there is an interruptor and a person who accedes to the interruption. The person being interrupted need not acquiesce. She or he should continue speaking, or calmly state, "You interrupted me. I haven't finished speaking yet."

2. If, when attempting to initiate or develop a topic, one member of the dyad receives only minimal responses from the other, the first speaker might revise his or her questioning strategies by asking increasingly more open questions.

For example, if, when one speaker asks, "Was the stock merger successful?" she receives a minimal "Uh huh," rather than asking further bi-polar (yes-no questions, or direct questions; e.g., "How did it go?" "Fine."), she should ask instead, "What aspects of your presentation were most well received?"

3. Both female and male listeners need to be aware of the verbal and vocal encouragement they provide while someone is

speaking. When speakers feel that their listeners are distracted, or that attention is being withheld, they should stop their communicative attempt and identify the *disconfirming responses* they are receiving before the interaction continues.

Evelyn Sieburg and Carl Larson examined seven types of responses in which one speaker ignored some significant aspect of another speaker's message.[15] Although in their research Sieberg and Larson did not specifically investigate gender differences between speakers, based on our informal classroom studies, the following disconfirming behaviors frequently are present in mixed-sex dyads.

a. *the impervious response.* In the impervious response, the speaker's comment is ignored verbally and nonverbally. Women often complain that in a meeting, a suggestion that was ignored when they voiced it was later adopted enthusiastically when offered by a male colleague. Women, children, minorities, the aged, the handicapped—all the less powerful segments of our society—find their messages met, all too frequently, with impervious responses. The resultant feeling of being "invisible" is extremely frustrating.

b. *the interrupting response.* As we have discussed above, the interrupting response is also a negation of a speaker's communicative attempt. Sieberg and Larson identify as particularly disconfirming interruptions, those that are not prefaced by such injections as "I understand, however..."

c. *the irrelevant response.* The irrelevant response occurs when a listener makes a comment totally unrelated to what the other person was just saying. This is one of the ways more powerful members of a dyad or a group attempt to control the selection of topics and to dominate discussions.

d. *the tangential response.* Related to the irrelevant response is the tangential one. In this case, a speaker nominally acknowledges the other speaker's message, but then shifts the conversation in another direction of his or her own choosing. An example of this type of response follows:

Employee: "I'd like to talk with you about my upcoming promotion."

Employer: "Sure, I know you want a raise, but now you'd better concentrate on your current project so that we don't get backlogged."

e. *the impersonal response.* This refers to a generalized, intellectualized response to a speaker's message. An impersonal response may be a categorical assertion, such as the response of the manager in the following exchange:

Union Representative: "I think we should have day-care facilities available on the premises for children of employees."

Manager: "Women want it both ways. You can't be a good worker and a good mother. Something has to give."

f. *the ambiguous response.* In this kind of interaction, the respondent is intentionally vague and may be misleading the first speaker. For example:

Worker: "Am I next in line for a supervisory position?"

Manager: "Could be. I'm not really sure how these things work."

g. *the incongruous response.* In this exchange the verbal and nonverbal components of the respondent's message appear to contradict each other:

Client: "Are you upset that I'm late for my appointment?"

Practitioner: (shouting and banging on the desk) "No, *I'm* **not** upset."

All of these disconfirming responses disparage and discourage the communicative attempts of speakers, and foster and reinforce a power differential. We know of no formal study that attempts to examine the greater incidence of disconfirming responses in either sex, although clearly more research in the area is needed. Superiors have the power to "disconfirm" the messages of subordinates. All of us need to be able to identify and eliminate these behaviors if we are to have more harmonious personal and professional interactions.

IV. NONVERBAL COMMUNICATION

In July 1984, at the National Democratic Convention, Representative Geraldine Ferraro was the first woman to be nominated for the vice-presidency by a major American political party. Throughout the media coverage of this historic event, journalists remarked repeatedly that with a man and a woman on the ticket, the Democratic Party must be especially "careful" of its candidates' nonverbal communication. In the media's estimation, nonverbal behaviors, such as the use of space, posture, movement, touch, eye contact and facial expression, are factors significant enough to cause one to win or lose an election and to change the course of history. Let us examine this potent and often extremely subtle form of communication.

A. Space, or Bigger is Better.

In American culture, space is indicative of power and individuals who have command over greater amounts of territory have more power. While in different cultures the amount of personal space individuals need may vary, within cultures, the closer people feel to each other emotionally, the more they are likely to allow each other to be close in proximity.

Women and lower status persons take up less space than males and higher status persons. In addition, people of lower status cannot control others from entering the space available to them. The boss can enter the worker's space, lean on the employee's desk, or tower over the subordinate, while only at the supervisor's invitation can the subordinate enter into the supervisor's space. In public and in private, in the workplace and in the streets, women constantly have their space encroached upon.

Frank Willis performed studies in which he measured the initial distance set by an approaching person. He established that both sexes approach women more closely than they do men.[16] As with interruptions, when women's space is intruded upon, they are apt to acquiesce to the intrusion. According to Jeanette Silveira's research, when men and women walked towards each other on the sidewalk, in twelve out of nineteen cases, the woman moved out of the man's way.[17] In the animal kingdom and among human beings, subordinates yield space to dominants.

Women are taught to take up less space than men. They are taught to sit with their legs together and elbows to their sides, and to walk with smaller steps. Men sit and move expansively. While seated, they spread their legs and put their arms on the armrests of chairs. They walk with longer strides. We know that these stereotypical ways of moving are not anatomically based because men in the Orient, for example, sit with their legs as closely together as Western women. Yet among Americans, men who retreat into as little available space as they can may not be considered masculine, while women who sit, stand and walk with open movements may be regarded as unfeminine. As with the archetypes for gender differentiated speech, the feminine model is one of relative powerlessness.

Females are encouraged to sit and move in ways that exacerbate their spatial limiations. For example, women may sit, poised on the edge of a chair, eagerly leaning forward rather than expanding into all the space available to them. "Feminine" clothes also contribute to a nonverbal image of female weakness. Tight skirts and tight slacks restrict movement. High heels force women to take small steps.

Women and men must recognize that the amount of space that they occupy delivers a potent message about their relative power or powerlessness. We do not suggest that women or men intrude upon others' space or conduct themselves in so relaxed a fashion as to sprawl over a chair or put their feet up on a desk in the workplace. But we do advise that individuals guard against their own tentativeness. As with the refusal to accede to an interruption, women can refuse to have their space violated, and by standing their ground assert their presence nonverbally.

B. Height.

Height is also a nonverbal variable that may be manipulated, thereby either empowering or impeding an individual. We say, "I look up to you" to indicate respect or admiration. "Higher" like "bigger" is often used to mean "better," or "more" (as in "higher class," "high" opinion).

In hierarchies, the individual with greater power frequently is perceived as taller than he or she is. Paul R. Wilson reported that undergraduates who were asked to estimate the height of a man who was described as any one of five academic ranks increased their estimation of his height when his ascribed status was increased.[18]

Men are generally taller than women and because we expect taller people to be more powerful, they frequently use their height to their advantage. Traditional female facial expressions of coyness and flirtation may reinforce the height and power differential between the sexes. For example, women frequently tilt their heads to the side and look upward when talking to men. Although the head tilt is a gesture which indicates attentive listening in either sex, women are apt to employ this more frequently in mixed-sex pairs than men; thus reinforcing the notion that in addition to listening, the woman is looking up to the man.

However, tall women have not been encouraged to use their height to their advantage. In fact, tall women are generally made to feel embarrassed about their height. Rather than proudly "walking tall," the larger woman may feel awkward and insecure. In a world in which height equals power, and women are not supposed to be powerful, the taller woman may feel that she is aberrant and that, consequently, she will be unattractive to men who value weakness in a woman over strength. As a result, taller womem may attempt to diminish themselves, to slouch and round their shoulders so as to retreat into or occupy as little space as possible.

We must guard against using height to control or to influence. Superiors need not tower over subordinates in the workplace. Tall individuals should be encouraged neither to use their height in an intimidating fashion, nor to attempt to diminish themselves by denying their personal power. Power need not be used as power *over* others.

C. Touch; or Just a Friendly Pat on the Back?

Touch, like physical closeness, may be considered an expression of affection, support or sexual attraction. However, touch may be used to express and maintain an asymmetrical relationship as well as a reciprocal one. For example, as a gesture of comfort, the doctor may touch the patient, but the patient may not initiate contact with the doctor. Similarly, upon entering the elevator, the department head may pat the elevator operator on the back and inquire about the elevator operator's family. However, this apparently "friendly" gesture is not as benign as it appears as long as the elevator operator does not have an equal right to initiate the same pat on the back and elicit similar personal information from the department head.

In 1970 and 1973, Nancy Henley performed observational studies investigating the relationship between touch and socioeconomic status, sex and age.[19] Henley found that higher status persons (individuals of higher socioeconomic status, male and older), touched lower status persons significantly more often. Henley's findings have important implications for both women and men. Individuals of both sexes should guard against using touch to assert authority. We should avoid initiating touch in situations where either the other individual is not desirous of the gesture, or where the higher status person would not wish their touch reciprocated.

But what about when the gesture *is* reciprocal? Women and men working together must be aware of outsiders possibly misconstruing the sexual implications of touch. In the Mondale-Ferraro campaign for the American presidency, newscasters mentioned that, distinct from previous campaigns in which the male candidates for president and vice-president traditionally linked inner arms and waved their raised outer arms, Mondale and Ferraro waved outer arms with their inner arms at their sides. They did not touch each other. In our opinion, it is unfortunate that either the same sex or opposite sex colleagues need to be circumspect with regard to genuine, reciprocal tactile demonstrations of support. However, the sexism and hetero-sexism in our society is such that, until people are accustomed to perceiving women as competent professionals in their own right, rather than as potential sexual objects, they will have difficulty imagining a collegial relationship between men and women absent of sexual implications. Consequently, at present, women and men who work together will continue to be subject to greater scrutiny than same sex pairs. All of us should guard against sexist and sex-role stereotyped interpretations of our own and each others' behavior.

D. Smiling; or Pleasing and being pleased.

From childhood, female children are admonished to smile. They are taught to smile not as an expression of their own pleasure, but because it is pleasing to others. The smile of appeasement is submissive behavior. Women are told that they are more attractive when they smile and appear happy. The key word in the previous sentence is "appear," for as long as women and other subordinates are concerned with pleasing others, they are not considered threatening to their superiors. The same may be said of Blacks and other minorities in America. As long as one *seems* to be satisfied with the position that has been allotted him or her, the hierarchical system is reinforced. Smiles, therefore, can function as genuine or as artificial signs of satisfaction.

In a number of service occupations, smiling is not preferred behavior, it is required. In Arlie Russel Hochschild's article entitled "Smile Wars; Counting the Casualties of Emotional Labor," the emotional labor required of stewardesses was discussed.[20] The stewardess, the waitress and the salesperson often pay a psychological price for their requisite smiles. When a smile is an *expected* part of the job, it becomes a commodity to be given. Women in these and other occupations frequently are required "to give" male patrons or superiors a smile. The constant feigned smile is an expression of duplicity. (And it must be feigned, for obviously no one can be happy all the time.) An individual engaging in this behavior cuts herself off from the expression of her own emotions. The smile becomes a mask, a form of "make up" constructed to gain the approval of one who has power. Subordinates are expected to smile at superiors. When the boss walks into the room, the secretaries are expected to smile and warmly greet him or her.

However, dominant members of a hierarchy are less likely to smile. They withhold verbal and nonverbal expressions of emotions. Instead, they are encouraged to appear neutral, impassive and to disclose as little about themselves as possible. Rather than smiling to gain others' approval, superiors are apt to assume facial expressions which imply that they are judging others.

One such example, according to Gerald I. Nierenberg and Henry H. Calero, is the disapproving attitude conveyed by raised eyebrows, a partially twisted head, and a look of doubt.[21] (In fact, the word *supercilious*, which comes from Latin, originally meant disdain or haughtiness as expressed by raising the eyebrows.)[22]

In the workplace, smiling should not be employed as an expression of a power differential. Women and other subordinates should evaluate the need to engage in overeager smiles for approval, or to offer smiles that are exacted from them. Men and dominant members of hierarchies should also reevaluate their tendency to equate smiling with compliance due them. They might also allow themselves to engage more openly in genuine mutual expressions of pleasure and approval.

E. Eye Contact.

Direct eye contact between two individuals may be interpreted in several different ways. Looking directly into another person's eyes can connote an aggressive threat, a sexual invitation, or a desire for honest and open communication.

Several years ago, actor Robert DeNiro, in the film *Taxi Driver*, portrayed a psychopathic murderer. Posed in front of a mirror, DeNiro glinted at his own reflection, taunting an imaginary assailant whom he envisioned to be staring at him. Menacingly, he asked, "...You talkin' to me? Who do you think you're talkin' to?" DeNiro's character interpreted a glance as an attempt at dominance. Researchers P.C. Ellsworth, J.M. Carlsmith and A. Henson tell us that a stare may have this function.[23] Ellsworth, et al. have reported studies that relate staring in humans to primate threat displays. For most individuals, a glance which catches another person's eye for several seconds is relatively insignificant. If, however, eye contact is maintained beyond several seconds, a nonverbal power contest may ensue in which the person with less power ultimately averts her or his eyes. In a number of cultures, children are taught that to look adults in the eyes is a sign of disrespect. Submission is indicated by a bowed head and an averted glance. In mixed sex pairs, women are more likely than men to avert their eyes.

Although persons of both sexes generally look at others more while listening than while speaking, studies by Ralph Exline, David Gray and Dorothy Schuette indicate that women engage in more mutual glances than men.[24] It may be conjectured that because of women's traditional dependency on male approval, they maintain eye contact in order to monitor visual cues of reinforcement. A person of superior status is not required to be as visually attentive as a subordinate.

In her book *Body Politics*, Nancy Henley attempts to differentiate between subordinate attentiveness and dominant staring. Henley claims that women, and other subordinates look at others more, but avert their eyes when looked at. Both of these behaviors are indicative of submissiveness.[25]

In any discussion of nonverbal communication, it is important not to interpret behavior in an ethnocentric fashion. Eye contact, like all other nonverbal behavior, has different connotations in different cultural contexts. There are cultures in which direct eye contact between men and women is regarded as a sexual invitation. For individuals from these backgrounds, averting one's eyes in a mixed sex dyad may be a sign of respect, modesty or disinterest, rather than inattentiveness or submissiveness. Because of differing expectations and interpretations for behavior, there is the potential for much misunderstanding in cross-sex and cross-cultural communication exchanges. Women and men need to be able to identify very precisely those behaviors which seem intrusive or inappropriate.

We are often unaware of our nonverbal behavior, and of how it is being interpreted by others. This can present obstacles in professional as well as personal settings. Certainly one can not work effectively if being ogled or ignored, leered at or laughed at. We need to monitor our own behavior responsibly, and to provide feedback to others about what we perceive to be their reactions to us.

SUMMARY

This chapter explored differences between the ways both sexes communicate. We examined such vocal differences as women's more precise articulation, higher pitch and rising intonation. We discussed verbal constructs such as tag questions, compound requests and individual words that are more prevalent in women's usage than in men's. We explored differences in the ways both sexes listen and respond to each other.

Finally, we identified differences in the ways men and women use space, height, touch, gestures and eye contact.

In all cases, the behaviors that have been designated as stereotypically female are those that are considered less powerful than the conventional male forms.

We hope that readers will become increasingly aware of the behaviors they manifest. Only then can we call into question the positive or negative evaluations which have been ascribed to gender differentiated communication styles and thereby have a richer repertoire from which to draw.

SUGGESTED ACTIVITIES

A. Focus on Listening.

Rousseau's quotation, which prefaces this chapter, motivated Mary Wollstonecraft in 1791 to write her historic *Vindication of the Rights of Woman* in rebuttal.

Whereas Rousseau enjoined women by "art" or artifice to render themselves agreeable to men, Wollstonecraft wished:

> ...to persuade women to endeavor to acquire strength, both of mind and body, and to convince them that *the soft phrases,* susceptibility of heart, delicacy of sentiment and refinement of taste, *are almost synonymous with epithets of weakness, and that those beings who are only the objects of pity* and that kind of love, which has been termed its sister, *will soon become objects of contempt.*   [emphasis added]
>
> Mary Wollstonecraft
> Introduction to First Edition
> *A Vindication of the Rights of Woman*

Observe individuals who employ the self-trivializing gestures and speech patterns identified in this chapter as mechanisms for making themselves agreeable, or to gain the approval of their superiors. Using the following chart, enter the strategies used and whether their superiors respond in the desired fashion, or dismiss the communication with "pity" or, as Wollstonecraft claims, with "contempt."

Speaker	Message Intended	Strategy Employed	Listener	Listener's Reaction

B. Focus on Dyadic Communication.

In pairs, role play an imaginary dialogue between Rousseau and Wollstonecraft or contemporary equivalents like Marabel Morgan and Gloria Steinem. Switch roles and attempt to defend the opposite position.

C. Focus on Small Group Communication: Interpersonal

In a small group, with equal numbers of male and female members, discuss a controversial social topic in front of an audience. For the purpose of the exercise, all the male members should employ the traditional feminine strategies (e.g., tag questions, qualifiers, disclaimers, etc.) and the female members should use categorical assertions and other masculine styles. After the discussion, ask the class or seminar group to evaluate the members according to the following criteria:

	Agree			Disagree	
	1	2	3	4	5

1. Member was an effective speaker.
2. Member was an effective listener.
3. Member seemed well prepared.
4. Member seemed authoritative.
5. Member seemed sensitive to communicative behavior of other group members.

D. Focus on Small Group Communication: Height and Power Differential.

In the midst of a conversation in an informal setting with a group of friends or family members, situate yourself at a different height than your companions. If everyone is sitting in chairs, sit on the floor, or stand up. Maintain your part of the conversation. Note people's nonverbal reactions to you. How long does it take until someone else in the group is "on your level?"

D. Focus on Communication: Exercises to Lower Pitch.

To open up and speak from the lower range of your natural pitch, practice by sitting in a chair and placing a book on the floor in front of you. Lean over limply, with your head between your legs, and read aloud into the floor. Tape yourself in this position. You will hear yourself speaking from the bottom reaches of your voice. Try to maintain this while in an upright position.

In order to maintain the lower pitch, place your hand low on your chest while you speak. By focusing your concentration lower in your chest instead of in a constricted throat, you will remind yourself to bring your pitch down.

Footnotes

[1]Roger W. Shuy, Walter A. Wolfram and William K. Riley, *Linguistic Correlates of Social Stratification in Detroit Speech.* Final Report, Project 6-1347, Washington, D.C.: U.S. Office of Education, 1967.

[2]William Labov, *Sociolinguistic Patterns,* (Philadelphia: University of Pennsylvania Press, 1973), pp. 243; 301-304.

[3]Peter Trudgill, "Sex, Covert Prestige and Linguistic Change in the Urban British English of Norwich" in Thorne and Henley.

[4]Walter Wolfram, *A Sociolinguistic Description of Detroit Negro Speech*, Washington, D.C.: Center for Applied Linguistics, 1969.

[5]Trudgill, "Sex, Covert Prestige and Linguistic Change in the Urban British English of Norwich," p. 91.

[6]Ignatius Mattingly, "Speaker Variation and Vocal Tract Size." Paper presented at Acoustical Society of America, 1966. Abstract in *Journal of the Acoustical Society of America,* 39 (1966), 1219.

[7]Jacqueline Sachs, Phillip Lieberman and Donna Erickson, "Anatomical and Cultural Determinants of Male and Female Speech," in Roger W. Shuy and Ralph W. Fasold, eds. *Language Attitudes: Current Trends and Prospects,* (Washington, D.Ċ.: Georgetown University Press, 1973), pp. 74-84.

[8]William Austin, "Some Social Aspects of Para Language," *Canadian Journal of Linguistics,* 11 (1965), 31-39.

[9]Ruth Brend, "Male-Female Intonation Patterns in American English," in Thorne and Henley, *Language and Sex,* pp. 84-87.

[10]Robin Lakoff, *Language and Women's Place,* (New York: Harper and Rowe Publishers, 1975), p. 17.

[11]Ibid., p. 15.

[12]Ibid., p. 10.

[13]Don H. Zimmerman and Candace West, "Sex Roles, Interruptions and Silences in Conversation," in Thorne and Henley.

[14]Fred L. Strodtbeck, Rita M. James and Charles Hawkins, "Social Status in Jury Deliberations," *American Sociological Review,* 22 (1957), 718.

[15]Evelyn Sieburg and Carl Larson, "Dimensions of Interpersonal Response," Paper presented to the International Communication Association, Phoenix, Arizona, 1971.

[16]Frank Willis, Jr. "Initial Speaking Distance as a Function of the Speakers' Relationship," *Psychonomic Science,* 5 (1966), 221-222.

[17]Jeanette Silveira, "Thoughts on the Politics of Touch," *Women's Press* (Eugene, Oregon), 1 (February, 1972), 13.

[18]Paul A. Wilson, "Perceptual Distortion of Height as a Function of Ascribed Academic Status," *Journal of Social Psychology,* 74, (1968), 97-102.

[19]Nancy Henley, "Power, Sex and Nonverbal Communication," in Thorne and Henley, *Language and Sex,* p. 193.

[20]Arlie Russell Hochschild, "Smile Wars: Counting the Casualties of Emotional Labor," *Mother Jones,* December 1983, pp. 35-42.

[21]Gerald I. Nierenberg and Henry H. Calero, *How to Read a Person Like a Book,* (New York: Hawthorne, 1971; Pocket Books, 1973), pp. 142-143.

[22]*Webster's New Twentieth Century Dictionary,* unabridged, 2nd edition, (New York: Simon and Schuster, 1980), p. 1828.

[23]Phoebe C. Ellsworth, J. Merrill Carlsmith and A. Henson, "The Stare as a Stimulus to Flight in Human Subjects: A Series of Field Experiments," *Journal of Personality and Social Psychology,* 21 (1972), 302-11.

[24]Ralph Exline, David Gray and Dorothy Shuette, "Visual Behavior in a Dyad as Affected by Interview Content and Sex of Respondent," *Journal of Personality and Social Psychology,* 1 (1968), 205.

[25]Nancy Henley, *Body Politics: Power, Sex and Nonverbal Communication,* (Englewood Cliffs, N.J.: Prentice-Hall, 1977), p. 163.

Chapter III

PROFESSIONAL IMAGE
A Key to Success

I practice hiding my anger.
My lips pout. I permit
old men to kiss me. I seem
eager. I offer. I sit
on their committee; I take
notes. I fold my hands. I keep
quiet when they speak
of what they use to keep me
busy, keep me quiet, smiling, out
of trouble. Their eyes mining me
are old. They try to find my danger,
but they cannot see this paper
is overheating, is about
to burst into flames.

Joan Larkin

In Chapter II, we discussed how male and female stereotypes are manifested. From the time we are born, these communication differences also affect our future professional aspirations and conform to the cultural expectations of our society. The impact of the media—television in particular—adds yet another layer to possible goals and prescribed roles for boys and girls and supports traditional modes of behavior. Television not only presents the stereotyped professional norm. We can see and hear how members of a particular profession are expected to talk and behave. In other words, we get a tube-size view of professionalism.

Two examples come to mind. On television law enforcement officials are usually depicted as casually-dressed males. Their use of language is largely informal, and through their body language we may associate these men with quick reflexes and brute strength. The medical doctor as depicted in most television series is also a man. He dresses in the requisite hospital "whites." His language usage is more formal and standard, and through verbal and nonverbal behavior, we may associate this individual with a quick intellect and manual dexterity.

By using males to portray members of these professions, the media reinforces the assumption that with rare exception, these two professions are the purview of men. Once a stereotype is created — whether positive or negative — it becomes extremely difficult to change our *perception* of how we should function.

The resistance of stereotypes to change can be demonstrated when we consider the trait of assertiveness, which is one of the requisite characteristics of the law enforcement official. Assertiveness is defined in part as driving, forceful energy or initiative. This is required of police officers who must both enforce the law and protect society from wrongdoers. Consequently, if assertiveness is regarded as an important aspect of the officers' professional image, what implications does this have for women within this profession?

If society ascribes assertiveness to a male mode of communication, and if assertiveness is also a trait necessary for police officers, it will generally be assumed that men will be more successful in that profession. This perception persists regardless of how assertive men or women actually are. Therefore, if women want to enter an occupation that requires traits and attitudes that fall into a stereotyped male paradigm of behavior, they must take greater pains to allay skeptics' fears and overcome the persistent male image that has dominated certain fields in American culture. This is no easy task, but it *has* been accomplished, and accomplished well in certain sectors of our society. In many areas, both men and women are able to bring to their positions their own special talents, and can learn to expand their effective communication potential from members of the opposite sex.

For *either* sex to succeed, or to project an image appropriate for their chosen field, it is important to understand the expectations associated with a given profession. It is important to learn a communication style—both verbal and nonverbal—that will lead to success and to personal fulfillment.

In the second chapter, the realities and dimensions of sex-stereotyped verbal and nonverbal behavior were discussed. We will now focus on how both sexes can use their prescribed behavior and environment to best professional advantage, and how they can incorporate the most functional traits of the opposite sex. Here we will present techniques and strategies that are not gender-specific and are equally applicable to both women and men.

I. VERBAL COMMUNICATION IN THE PROFESSIONAL SETTING

Verbal interaction on a one-to-one basis and in group situations within the professional framework, has been the object of considerable research and interpretation during the past two decades. At first, findings related almost exclusively to men in such situations, because the number of men in professions far exceeded the number of women.

A shift in the attitudes of and towards women entering a broader spectrum of professional endeavors, opened the door to employment for many. The *perception of* and *attitude toward* the communication differences between women and men have sparked the emergence of research, articles, books, courses, even programs of study, devoted to the implicit and the explicit dimensions of gender in American culture. Our concern here is how male and female behavior affect the professional in different communication contexts. We will explore mechanisms for both sexes to "borrow" from each other and to strengthen their own communication capabilities.

Generally there are three broad interpersonal contexts within our daily and our professional lives. They are the one-to-one dyad, the group setting or meeting, and the public speaking forum. These contexts require strong communication skills.

Contrary to the myth, speakers are made; they need not be "born." Improvement in performance in all of the above settings *can* be achieved through knowledge, understanding, and practice.

A. One-To-One Dyad.

One-to-one interaction is the most common interpersonal context in professional settings—particularly in the service professions.

If we return to the two examples cited at the beginning of this chapter—law enforcement officials and physicians—we see that how these two groups function in a dyadic setting is a crucial part of their overall effectiveness. As mentioned earlier, the majority of these two groups are men, although women are now entering all careers in unprecedented numbers. The two communication skills used most commonly are listening and speaking. *Yet,* studies indicate that men do not listen effectively to less powerful segments of the population, particularly the poor, the aged, children, and women.[1] The refusal or inability to listen can have considerable impact on these populations; which can range from a constant source of frustration to the individuals not taken seriously, to a possible life-threatening situation.

Officers and physicians represent authority figures in this culture. If the poor, the aged, women and children stereotypically represent the weaker and more dependent segments of our society—again a product of cultural expectations—the gap between the male professionals and the populations they serve may be extensive.

The male professionals in this instance should implement measures to *close* this cultural and sociological communication gap. The professional must *encourage* communication from others. The physician should ask probing questions. S/he must be certain the patient fully understands every question. S/he must allow the patient to respond to his/her questions and to have the patient ask questions of his or her own—without feeling pressured, rushed, or inadequate. Because the ability to nurture, to demonstrate patience, is culturally encouraged in women, the female physician may have in her own upbringing the strategies for fostering communication with her patients.

The male police officer, when taking a report from an elderly victim, or from a woman, should avoid stereotyping the victim as "hysterical," or "out-of-control." Such labels tend to result in regarding the information as less accurate or as less important. As with physicians, officers need to listen empathetically and avoid preconceived judgements about the populations they serve.

In the examples presented above, the communication exchange is between superordinate and subordinate. When communication exchanges are between colleagues of different genders, other problems may surface. The distinctions between nonverbal and verbal behavior between the sexes have been explained in Chapter II. These differences are evident even when men and women are in the same profession. The differences themselves have little meaning until we *assign* a value or judgement to the behavior. The judgement leads to stereotypes — powerful labels attached to a group of individuals. These labels and our attitudes toward them are hard to change.

Potential conflicts between women and men can arise when there are discrepancies between the values assigned to male and female behavior as evidenced by the women who have shared some of their experiences with us.

— A female attorney hired by a prestigious firm discovered that the partner to whom she was assigned expected sexual favors in return for her advancement in the firm.

— A female resident physician who smiled and often joked with other residents or attendants was regarded as a flirt trying to get special treatment in the hospital.

— A female administrator would meet another female administrator at the office coffee machine a couple of times during the week to take a break and to discuss informally office problems with her colleague. She was accused of wasting valuable company time "chatting" with her friend.

— A female professor had to miss an important meeting because her child fell ill. She was considered not to be committed seriously to her profession.

— An attractive nurse was hired by a hospital. Others whispered that she went into nursing in order to "catch" a doctor for a husband.

—When a woman dentist was invited to address other
dentists at a major convention, the content of her speech
was not regarded as important as the lectures given by her
male colleagues.

—A recent M.B.A. graduate was hired by a large corporation to head a division. She was described as "pert,"
"cute," and "unable to negotiate herself out of a paper
bag" — *before* her first day of work.

These examples illustrate, but by no means exhaust, the
kinds of damaging stereotyping that occur within the professions. Certainly it is not hard to understand *why* this occurs. If
the professional sector of our culture has existed for so long
based on a male model of communication, any behavior that
may be construed as *deviating* from that model may be considered as suspect, less worthy, or a threat.

For those women who have worked very hard to achieve a
particular professional status, the answer to stereotyping is
not simply to start behaving like a man. Such a response is unnatural, debilitating, and often leads to the unfortunate opposite types of stereotyping: that a woman is "pushy,"
"aggressive," a "ball-buster," "masculine," "frustrated," and
so on.

How women can succeed in the professional dyad is not
something that can be neatly prescribed. Successful professional interaction with men often requires testing certain communication strategies. It involves understanding one's own personality strengths and weaknesses. For example, if a woman is
shy, she will need to practice communicating more openly with
others in order to overcome this trait in the business world. A
woman who has always allowed men to interrupt her or to take
charge in social situations will have to discourage such interruptions when dealing with male colleagues. A woman who in
social situations will often touch men and allow men to touch or
embrace her, may find such tactile behavior in the office to be
considered suspect and open to rumor. Finally, if a woman
finds herself the target of sexual harrassment, unless she is
able to sidestep the situation, or is resolved to leave her position, she must decisively object to such advancements *as soon
as* they become manifest. (Waiting for this type of behavior to
stop, or hoping the man will lose interest is more often than not
wishful and erroneous thinking.)

B. Group Interaction.

The small-group meeting is the second most commonly employed method of communication within an organization or within an institution. It can be used to report or to present information, to elicit information, to "brainstorm" or to solve problems, to mediate, arbitrate, and to discipline. While it is expected that all members of a group will cooperate, and that they will endeavor to maintain the integrity and the purpose of the meeting, the primary responsibility for assuring an effective and efficient meeting remains with the chair.

As we have seen in the previous chapter, a strong speaking style and assertive nonverbal behavior are the stereotyped domain of male speakers, while a less self-assured manner of speaking and reticent body language are more typical of female behavior. Stereotypical female behavior, therefore, may not be conducive to a leadership communication mode. It may not be conducive to chairing or running a meeting.

However, because women are entering positions of authority in business and industry in increasing numbers, they will probably be required to participate in and to chair meetings during their careers. The ability to assume such responsibilities is not easy to develop. Avoiding the stereotypically "weak" verbal and nonverbal behavior discussed in Chapter II is one step towards reaching a more assertive communication style. But there are additional techniques and strategies for conducting a meeting that cross over gender lines. Those men who may be poor listeners, confrontative, or overpowering in their communication style, might be able to dominate or control a meeting, but would not be able to conduct a *productive* one. Men, too, could therefore benefit from being aware of the strategies for leading a group.

The structure of any meeting and how it is run largely determine its success or failure. When setting up a meeting, it is important to remember that formats may vary. The leader should make certain that the format is appropriate to the issues involved. For example, if an emergency requires that a meeting be convened to solve a particular problem, we would expect involvement from the members, and a collaborative focus would be appropriate. This is distinct from the type of meeting in which different members might be asked to present reports. In such cases of information sharing, a high level of taking turns is warranted, and less interrupting would be anticipated.

There are five basic points the group leader must keep in mind in order to ensure a successful meeting. The first three points deal with *planning* the meeting.

1. *Time.*

When scheduling a meeting, the chair should allow for sufficient time. The emphasis is on *sufficient.* There are complaints at both ends of the time scale when this dimension is overlooked. Keeping people at a meeting for two hours when one hour is more than sufficient to complete the agenda is just as frustrating to those involved as not allowing enough time to address the issues.

2. *Agenda.*

The chair should plan a careful agenda and include only those items that are germane to the purpose and to the focus of the meeting and that can be realistically and adequately covered within the allocated time frame.

3. *Preparing the group.*

The chair should prepare her- or himself and the other members of the meeting. It is advisable to circulate the agenda among the participants well in advance. If members are expected to make a report at the meeting, their name should be so designated next to the topic assigned to them. This written confirmation should be preceeded by a phone call so that the length and focus of the presentation can be determined.

These three steps are particularly important for women who chair meetings with both sexes in attendance. If women are not generally as assertive as men in the business setting, they can strengthen control over the process itself by paying careful attention to planning a meeting.

4. *Environment.*

The environment, or where a meeting is held, is the fourth element in establishing a meeting. There are four basic considerations for determining where a meeting should be held.

a) *Territory* or the *appropriateness* of the facility to the tone of the meeting should not be ignored. Whether a meeting is formal or informal may be dependent on the location. A formal grievance, for example, may require a space different from the kind of facility used for a "brainstorming" session. Careful attention should be paid to the comfort and appropriateness of the environment to all of the group members. For example, business meetings that are informally scheduled after hours at the pub or golf course may prevent women's equal participation.

b) *Privacy* is often a critical element of any meeting. The desired outcome of most meetings is either to resolve issues or problems, or to share important information and generate new ideas. Since much of what results from a meeting arises at the time the meeting takes place, a lack of interruptions and distractions facilitates this process. Nothing short of an emergency should require the interruption of a meeting in progress.

c) *Round tables* are desirable in meetings where a collaborative effort of collegial exchange is desired. A round table connotes a more equal relationship among the members at a meeting and enhances a cooperative spirit. This is of particular importance when men and women are participating because it eliminates the distinction of status that is created when an individual sits at the head of a table.

d) The aesthetic and physical *comfort* of a facility affects the meeting process because members can focus on the substance at hand rather than on whether or not the temperature, for example, is comfortable.

5. *The Chairperson.*

The role of the chairperson or group leader is the final consideration when conducting a meeting. The chairperson is in a position of authority. Because of this ascribed power, women who may be perceived as less authoritative may be regarded as less effective in this role. Men, who may be perceived as dogmatic, may be regarded as overbearing in a position of power. To overcome these stereotypes, it is incumbent upon both sexes to be aware of how they may be perceived, and to take the following five steps to maximize their effectiveness.

a) The first responsibility of the chair is to assure that the purpose of the meeting is not violated. The chair must assume responsibility for following the agenda and for allowing sufficient time for each specified issue.

b) Second, the leader should maintain an objective attitude throughout the meeting. This is especially crucial when there is disagreement among the participants. In instances when there is disagreement, the leader should invite feedback from *all* members so that the different sides of the issues are well represented. If one member is dominating the discussion, the chair might interrupt and encourage reactions from the quieter members of the group. Following a heated discussion or conflict, it is helpful for the leader to summarize all of the issues presented or raised, and perhaps to suggest areas for future thought or discussion.

c) A third function of the chair is to be flexible and to exercise good judgement. There is nothing more frustrating than to be in the middle of an exciting and stimulating discussion on an important topic when the leader decides that solely because of time, the members must move on to the next item on the agenda. A strong group leader will be sensitive to how the meeting is progressing, and she or he should exercise discretion when staying with, leaving, or even introducing a new topic at a meeting.

d) Delegation of tasks is the fourth area where group leaders can affect the meeting's success. Most meetings are regularly scheduled and are attended by the same participants. The monthly Board Meeting, the bi-monthly Directors' Meeting, and the weekly Executive Meeting are some examples. In meetings of this type, materials or reports are often required. It is important for the leader to be able to delegate assignments to the participants. Many leaders or chairs believe they should do and prepare everything themselves. Not only can this become an overwhelming burden for one individual, it also discourages the creative and possibly thoughtful output of members.

The types of tasks assigned to members should be done *regardless* of gender. We have continually seen the woman present assigned the responsibilities of taking minutes, making the phone calls, and ordering food. It is routinely taken for granted that all women can type and are adept in these areas, and they are consequently assigned the "nuisance" tasks. Rarely are such tasks given to men to perform (unless *only* men are in attendance). The chair's responsibility for designating

appropriate, fair, and nonsexist assignments should not be
minimized. It is important to keep in mind that we often equate
capability with level of assignments and performance. Women
who are continually assigned and who accept what are considered menial tasks, stand to lose professional recognition.

e) The final responsibility often required of the leader or the
chair is *feedback* following the meeting. By summarizing decisions made, and by indicating topics delegated or assigned for
future discussion, the leader is clarifying what transpired, and
is confirming as well everyone's expectations for subsequent
meetings.

It is clear from what has been presented here, that preparing for and running a meeting require a great deal of organization, thought, sensitivity, and discretion. It should be pointed
out as well that these traits are *not* limited to either men or to
women. Both sexes can and should be competent in conducting
a meeting, for in fact, most organizations thrive on the outcome
of such interactions.

C. Public Communication in Professional Settings

Public communication or public speaking is the third and
final example of communication within a professional framework. For many, it is fortunate that this type of communication
is the least frequently employed method, because the idea of
speaking before an audience can cause immense fear.

However, individuals, regardless of whether or not they
have a high-visibility career, may at some point in their lives
find themselves at a podium or in front of an audience. A police
officer may speak to a group of teen-aged youths about the
dangers of driving while intoxicated. A parent can find him- or
herself in front of the local school board, seeking approval of
funds for after-school activities for the children. An attorney
may make his or her case before a jury. A physician may be
asked to present his or her findings regarding the use of a particular surgical technique to a group of peers at a national convention. A director of marketing may be required to convince
his or her colleagues and superiors that an expenditure of
millions on a new product will result in high profits for the firm.
The possibilities and potential situations requiring an indi-

vidual to speak in public are limitless, and speech communication courses around the country are filled with students and
professionals who recognize the need to become proficient
public speakers.

We mentioned before that speaking is a learned activity, and
that speakers can be taught to improve. This is especially true
for the public speaker. As with the other communication contexts, gender is a factor in the public speaking forum. There
are four important factors to consider when speaking in public.
They are: the audience, the environment, the image of the
speaker, and the speech itself.

1. *Audience.*

All speakers need to engage in a thorough analysis of their
audience before they even begin to prepare their message. This
is especially true of women and others who assume that their
messages might be resisted by those whom they will address.
To maximize their chances of success, the prospective speaker
must ask the following:

a) What does this audience already know or believe about
the topic? The audience's level of expertise and attitude
toward the subject are vital guides to help the speaker adapt
the speech to the audience.

b) What does the audience already know or believe about the
speaker? How one demonstrates his/her credibility will have
an enormous effect on how the message is received.

c) How does the audience feel about the environment/occa-
sion? Is it uncomfortable, somber, festive? All of these affect
the tone one takes with a group.

d) How does the group identify itself? What are the areas of
commonality for audience members? Successful speakers
identify issues in common with the audience and so are more
likely to be perceived as one of them.

2. *Environment.*

A major source of fear of speaking in public stems from the
fact that the factors over which we want the *most* control, are
those very factors over which we have no or very little control.
An invited speaker is out of his or her territory. She or he
enters a new or foreign environment and the unknown factors
often contribute to stagefright. While it is impossible to control

or to regulate all of the elements within an environment, some information can be obtained ahead of time.

The type of space or facility in which the speaking engagement will occur is of utmost importance. Will the speaker be in a lecture hall, a board room, or a classroom? Will the event occur in a gazebo, at a park, etc.? The size and the nature of the facility will undoubtedly affect how formal or informal the speaking context will be, and will influence how the speaker prepares her- or himself: from what to wear, to the type of body language and gestures practiced, even to some extent, to the content and length of the speech itself.

For example, speaking outdoors will limit the use of audio-visual materials. Speaking in an intimate setting will obviate the need for an elaborate microphone set-up. A room with uncomfortable seating may cause a speaker to reduce the time of the speech. And a room with sophisticated equipment may encourage the use of the electronic media during the speech.

Ideally, the speaker should visit the speaking site well in advance of the engagement. This would enable the speaker to make the kinds of determinations and revisions suggested above during the speech-planning phase. When this is not possible, as is most often the case, the speaker should ask for detailed information, and, if possible, for a sketch of the facility.

3. *The Image of the Speaker.*

The image of the speaker — who she or he is and how well he or she speaks, often has more of an impact on the success or failure of a speaking engagement than the content of the speech itself. In Chapter II we discussed briefly the importance of being perceived as a credible speaker. Speakers generally are considered credible when they demonstrate their competence, expertise, reliability, dynamism, and co-orientation with their audience. Nonetheless, there are still those who doubt the credibility of female speakers in professional settings.

It is therefore of particular importance to women to be able to anticipate the resistances of their audience in advance in order to address and overcome them. Otherwise, the audience's attitude toward the speaker may continue to be an obstacle.

For example, a female mechanic demonstrating a technical skill to male colleagues needs to address within her speech any resistance she anticipates. She might preface her remarks with a statement such as: "Perhaps you are wondering what I, a woman, might be able to teach you about auto mechanics. In the five years that I apprenticed and assisted others before opening up my own chain of garages, I discovered..." In other words, the speaker has acknowledged and overcome the audience's possible negative opinion before they were able to solidify it. In addition, by mentioning her expertise, she has bolstered her credibility.

As with all aspects of communication, public speaking has its verbal and nonverbal components. Both of these dimensions often become exaggerated in a public speaking situation because of the large distance between the speaker and the audience. Fortunately, the speaker can control the majority of the important aspects of presenting oneself verbally and nonverbally.

a) *Putting your best voice forward.* There are four aspects of delivery over which individuals have control. How *loudly* one speaks is critical to being a good public speaker, because the best speech, if unheard, cannot be effective. Most speakers are able to project and modulate their voice levels with little difficulty or undue strain. But for those situations where the facility is too big, or the audience too large, an amplification system will enable the speaker to reach the audience.

The *rate of delivery* is the second verbal element which speakers are able to control. Most speakers tend to speak much too quickly. Practicing the speech and placing appropriate comments in one's notes *reminding* the speaker to slow down are two techniques that can enable the speaker to be clearly and adequately understood by the audience. The chances are good that if the speaker thinks he or she is speaking too slowly, he or she has probably achieved a good pace for those listening.

Rhythm and *conversational style* form the third and fourth elements of voice control and they are closely related. The rhythm of the speech should be appropriately varied; the speaker should avoid delivering the speech in a monotone voice. Also, the style of delivery should be as conversational as is appropriate for the occasion.

The three remaining verbal areas are those over which the speaker has less control. One's pitch and voice quality are largely a product of environment, social, and biological development, and therefore more resistant to change. However, vocal and breathing exercises can help to alter these two traits within certain limitations. For women who are negatively stereotyped for possessing a voice that is too "breathy" or too much like a "little girl," facilitating a change in vocal quality can make a difference in how they are received as public speakers.

b) *How you are perceived affects how you are received.* The final area over which public speakers have limited control is how they are *received* and *perceived* by an audience. In this regard, gender strongly affects an audience and can influence them *regardless* of the speech content and delivery. This circumstance, as revealed in the first chapter, has had a debilitating effect on women as speakers and on women in general. Unfortunately, recent studies indicate the individuals continue to form attitudes of others based on gender stereotypes.

Studies on a college campus revealed that when the *same* speech was delivered to a mixed-sex audience by a man and by a woman, the students believed the man's speech to be more accurate, and considered him to be a better speaker.[2] It is indeed difficult for women to compete with a cultural legacy of criticism and of not being taken seriously. But as more women *continue* to speak up and out, as more continue to enter the former professional domain that belonged to men, the likelihood that misperceptions will diminish are quite good.

What the speaker says *without* words is of great importance to the public speaking situation — and, in fact, to any communication exchange. Almost any movement at all possesses symbolic meaning.

Nonverbal communication should be appropriate to the speech and to the situation, and should develop naturally from the content. Eye contact should be established and sustained with as many members of the audience in different parts of the lecture hall so that the speaker's head and eyes move naturally. Posture should be relaxed — neither too stiff, nor too "laid back." And again, *appropriateness* for the occasion and for the audience should be the key here as well.

The speaker can and should exercise control over dress and body language. The Eakins and Eakins study cited on page 59 in this section reveal that physical appearance and gender may also affect audience affiliation and response. A person who is perceived as attractive will have an easier time being initially received by others. Thus, a favorable response to beauty influences the effect a public speaker has. A man perceived as good-looking is the most enthusiastically received public speaker in our society. A woman who is considered attractive may be warmly received as well, but it may be primarily for her looks and not for the veracity of her message. Men who are characterized as plain or as not-so-good-looking may receive high marks for authority when speaking. According to Eakins and Eakins, the least accepted speaker — from a reception and acceptance standpoint — is the woman considered to be plain.[3]

While trying to project oneself in the most effective manner possible should not be ignored, the format and content of the speech is of overriding importance for all speakers.

3. *Making Your Case: The Speech Act.*

The two most common purposes of public speaking are to inform and to persuade. In both cases, speakers hope to communicate complete, clear, well-thought-out messages; however, their general goals might differ.

The informative speaker attempts to impart information that she or he feels is objective and accurate. Speakers who attempt to be informative try to distance themselves from their biases about the subject at hand, and to report the facts. They aim to impart information that will be useful and/or of interest to their audience. Successful informative speakers develop major points that can be discussed adequately within time constraints, and that are at an appropriate level for their audience.

One technique that speakers often use to ascertain whether or not they have adequately and effectively communicated their message, is to invite audience feedback and response. Opening the floor to questions not only lets the speaker know if the message has been understood, it also helps to bring the speaker and the audience closer together, thereby bridging the communication gap which the public speaking format creates.

In contrast to the informative public communication context which aims to impart information, the purpose of persuasive public communication is to influence the values, attitudes and behavior of the listeners. The effective speaker does this by trying to get the audience "to affiliate" with him or her. Persuasive speakers accomplish this by identifying needs or problems that may exist for the audience, demonstrating the gravity of those needs, and attempting to convince the audience to accept the speaker's plan of action as the best possible way to satisfy their needs. For example, if a speaker wishes to encourage audience members to protest the nuclear arms build-up, he or she will have to explain how the existence of nuclear weaponry threatens *that particular audience*. Only if the listeners believe that *they* have a need that must be solved or satisfied will they be prompted to *do* something about the problem.

In Chapter I, we discussed Evelyn Fox Keller's contention that a pretense of objectivity may be based upon a specifically masculine archetype in which facts are valued over feelings. Traditionally, women have not been considered as objective and credible authorities as have men. Similarly, in conventional models of persuasive speaking, it is posited that a successful speaker must actively seek to change the attitudes, beliefs or behaviors of audience members. In this regard women are also at a disadvantage as they have not been encouraged to develop rhetorical styles that facilitate the imposition of their will over others.

In Chapter II, we considered the speaking style of women and the negative implications when women do not speak forthrightly and with self-assurance. In the public speaking setting, the ability to project a confident, assertive image becomes a requisite for success. The use of tag questions, particles, frequent pauses, and especially disclaimers, must be consciously banished from the speech delivery. While speaking in a professional manner may not eradicate audience bias when evaluating women and men speakers, any attempt to avoid the stigmatized female speech style will undoubtedly improve the image of professional women in society.

The speech is the tool through which the public speaker communicates his or her message. To succeed, the speaker must have a clear sense of what he or she wants to say, and must use the best methods for conveying this message to the audience. Women, who are aware that their gender may be an ever-present barrier to the speech act, will be even more cognizant of choosing everything — from facts to format, to clothes, and to body language — to achieve the highest possible level of audience affiliation and acceptance.

II. NONVERBAL ENVIRONMENT IN PROFESSIONAL SETTINGS

As either a consumer of professional services or as a professional offering services, it is important to understand that space, time, appearance and body language communicate a great deal about how we view ourselves, as well as about how we regard others. Used effectively, our environment can enhance our success. Ineffective use of the environment can be debilitating and can undermine our efforts.

If individuals recognize the need to improve and to master good verbal communication skills, it is equally important to recognize that these skills can only be effective in a nonverbal context that is neither negative nor destructive.

A. Space and Ambiance.

Edward T. Hall calls space a "hidden" dimension because normally we are not conscious of the space we inhabit until it is either violated or changed. Experiments conducted with animals have shown that taken to its extreme, space deprivation or misuse can lead to biological changes in the body that under certain circumstances can result in illness or death.[4]

While it is not likely that the office environment will produce such dire consequences, our culture often pays little attention to the impact of environment on both the individual performing a service who inhabits the environment, and on the person who enters the environment to obtain services. The impact of environment, however, may be considerable, and it therefore should not be ignored. A self-employed professional must inhabit an environment that is adequate in size and comfort. This will reduce tension and strain, and will create an atmosphere conducive to communication. From the point of view of the manager who must oversee the space where either colleagues or subordinates must function, the environment can be an important factor in sustaining or improving productivity. Like most nonverbal communication elements, space can be effectively controlled, manipulated and managed.

1. *Space as a status symbol.*

Status in organizations is often acknowledged by the size and placement of offices, and by the quality of furniture assigned to an individual. Generally, those with the most status have the greatest allocation of private territory within a hierarchy. These individuals are likely to be at a distance from the "public" or access space, protected by a bank of support individuals (e.g., the receptionist, the secretary, the assistant, etc.). And in a hierarchy where status is recognized, the furniture assigned to individuals possessing a high rank is likely to be more abundant and of better quality than the furniture customarily used in the organization.

One student who works for a major corporation, reported to us that the side chairs were used as one measure of status in the company. The secretaries had hard-back, armless, wooden chairs next to their desks. Office managers had similar chairs, but with arms. The account executives had leather chairs without arms, and the vice-presidents had leather chairs with arms.

In instances where titles do not so readily distinguish status and function, other markers of status and prestige may be used. Many large law firms, for example, assign offices (large vs. small; with or without windows), on the basis of length of service with the firm.

Gender and status in organizations are issues to the extent that even though increasing numbers of women are joining the professional ranks, the largest number of female employees still dominate the support service positions (i.e., clerk/typist, receptionist, secretary, etc.). Consequently, the use of space in organizations continues to reflect professional inequality between the sexes.

2. *Space as a sign of professionalism.*

When most individuals enter a professional environment, they expect a certain sense of style, a certain amount of decorum—what we call professional image. Many professionals, particularly those in private practice or in individually-owned and operated businesses, are sensitive to this expectation and they respond accordingly.

However, there are many individuals who *intend* to change their environment, but do not "get around to it." And there are still others who appear not to care about their workspace. Ignoring the professional environment may negatively affect the office's effective functioning and its success.

In an article on the communication environment for dental practitioners, Deborah Borisoff provides an example of the potential debilitating effect of a disorganized office on the dentist.[5] If a prospective new patient enters a professional office for the first time and finds a small, cluttered and physically uncomfortable waiting room that is in need of repair, this patient will probably form a negative impression of the practitioner. The visual cues of the environment are telling the prospective patient that the office is disorganized, that the practitioner perhaps is not concerned with the patient's comfort, and possibly, the dentist does not have a positive self-image because the physical aspects of the office are not maintained. Borisoff notes:

> Thus it is possible for the patient to have a negative opinion of the dentists before even meeting him/her because the patient has ascribed the physical attributes of the environment to the person who controls the environment. And this may lead to doubt or mistrust in the dentist's ability. While it is obvious that the dentist may in fact be very capable, he/she is at a disadvantage when he/she meets the prospective patient because he/she must overcome the negative image that the office has conveyed. And the dentist must work harder to do so.[6]

How we utilize the space we have is often one indication of communication style. While each profession has its own brand of acceptable communication, within the constraints is a certain degree of latitude where individuals can affect their environment.

For example, in any office, placing a desk between where the host and guest are seated creates a barrier — a physical one, which, depending upon the nature of the interaction, can become an emotional or psychological one as well. In addition, if the office is very large, the further the distance of the guest's chair form the desk, the greater the barrier becomes. Therefore, if it is beneficial for an individual to create and maintain a distance from those who visit the office, this physical distancing is one technique that will achieve this goal and create a formal environment.

In most day-to-day encounters, however, *facilitating* communication and *bridging* communication barriers are preferred goals. For example, male physicians have long been accused of not listening effectively; of not appearing to be sufficiently interested in their patients' concerns. Many physicians are aware of this negative stereotype, and are trying to alter this image. One way to do this is to de-formalize the consultation room. By bringing the patient physically closer to the doctor (i.e., by placing the chair *next* to the doctor's desk rather than in front of it), the removal of the physical barrier will help to create a positive communication environment — one in which, hopefully, both the patient and the physician will feel comfortable.

Another sign of communication within professional organizations and institutions is the office door. In some European cultures, (Germany is one example), the closed office door is standard operating procedure for office workers and does not impede or discourage interruptions. In American offices, however, the closed door stands for the desire or need for privacy; or indicates that a meeting may be in progress. We consider it good manners *not* to enter someone's office when the door is closed without first knocking or calling.

The concept of the closed door as a barrier to communication is especially important for men and women who are in positions that *require* interaction with colleagues, customers, or subordinates. Research indicates that within organizations, individuals are more inclined to approach female superordinates with a problem, than they are male bosses. One reason for this is that women are considered to be more nurturing and accessible in general than men, so that individuals are less reluctant to approach them.[7] Consequently, if men are in positions that demand open communication, their gender alone may be creating a barrier, regardless of how effective they are as communicators. It, therefore, becomes necessary for these individuals to make a special effort to overcome or decrease such obstacles to communication. One way would simply be to leave the office door open for a certain amount of time each day so that visitors could drop by freely to discuss various matters or problems. In such instances communication would be encouraged, and gender barriers diminished.

3. *Space and Support Staff Productivity*

If communication with the public is one goal of professional communication, communication with others *within* the professional environment should be of equal concern. The attitude and productivity of the support staff in any institution or organization are vitally important, usually forming a connection or link between the public and the professional worlds.

All too often the individuals in support positions—usually women—find that their office needs are overlooked or totally ignored. Because we are advocating space utilization and environment as important considerations in the work place, the facilities of the support staff should also be addressed. Those on the lower scale of the hierarchy, usually women (and also minorities), have the least amount of personal space. We have established that comfort within an organization can facilitate productivity. Thus it would behoove those in charge to consider the following points when planning a facility or assigning space to those in support positions.

a) Is the work space adequate for the employee to perform his/her job, allowing for enough space surrounding the desk or work space?

b) Is the work environment sufficiently quiet to allow for concentration on the tasks at hand?

c) Is the employee assigned some private space of his or her own, for example, to lock away personal items; to store one's own materials?

d) Are comfortable facilities available for employees to take a break during the day away from the work space?

It is only through a serious consideration of the value and function of space within any organization or institution that the dignity and productivity of those providing and of those receiving services can be truly enhanced.

B. Time in Professional Settings.

We normally regard time as a referential dimension. From consulting the clock, we typically know our daily routine: when to get up; when to leave for school or work; when to eat; when to arrive for appointments; and when to sleep. We might respond or react to time by proceeding more slowly or more quickly depending upon how much time we have to complete a prescribed task or chore.

However, in professional settings, time can take on quite a different meaning from the referential standpoint. Time can be manipulated. It can be used as a tool: to communicate information; to inspire fear; to invoke uncertainty; to create anger; or to demonstrate power. For example, if an individual is in a meeting with his or her superior, the superior has control over the time. After a certain period of time has elapsed, the superior might glance at his or her watch, or have the secretary interrupt the meeting. The superior might mention an impending meeting, or might stand up and thank the subordinate for coming to the meeting. Such examples represent common business practice and communicate the following: the meeting has run its course; the person in authority has indicated that the meeting is over. Time in this context is used as a marker — to signal that time has run out.

Being kept waiting for a meeting to commence may communicate other meanings of time. Often, how much time one individual waits for another is a function of the visitor's status. Within organizations, it is customary for the person having less authority to go to the office, to the "territory" of the person with more authority. A hierarchy is thus established by *where* the meeting is being held. Also, *when* the meeting will begin is controlled by the individual in power. While it is the prerogative of the person in power to control the time, judicious use of time is expected. Under normal operating procedures, no individual within an organization should be required to wait unduly to see another individual. What is considered a long time period will certainly vary in different cultural settings, organizations, or geographic regions. Generally, for Americans, waiting up to fifteen minutes is not out-of-line. However, waiting one hour without many explanations and apologies may show a lack of respect for the individual who is waiting.[8]

When we are the recipient of such manipulation, we respond emotionally because time used in such ways does *communicate* to us. We clearly understand the intended message that our time is not considered as valuable as that of the person who has kept us waiting. Consequently, time becomes another important means of nonverbal communication in our daily and in our professional lives.

The final example of control of time is when it is used as a commodity: the client or patient is buying the time and expertise of the professional (e.g., attorney, accountant, physician, dentist, etc.). A client or patient who is paying dearly for the services of a professional, may equate the services with time — especially the time it takes to set up an appointment in an emergency. Other ways that the perceived quality of care is affected by time include the time it takes in the waiting room facilities before seeing the professional, the time the professional spends with the patient or client without interruptions, and, in the cases of health-care specialists, the time allocated to discussing the patient's health following the examination.

In the case of health-care professionals, a violation of any of the aforementioned time frames may upset the patient, invoking impatience, frustration, and, at times, anger. The extent to which the patient is affected will depend upon his/her relative power and access to alternative treatment. Since any professional has a certain amount of control over his or her time, it is important for all professionals, but especially those in service positions, to make judicious decisions when it comes to scheduling appointments and to managing effectively and efficiently the time spent with clients or patients.

C. Appearance and Body Language

Professional appearance and body language are the areas where gender usually has the greatest impact. Traditionally, when we think of professional attire, we envision the uniform or clothing worn by the sex that dominates the profession. A nurse's uniform is usually associated with a woman. A police officer's uniform gives rise to a male image.

There are no conflicts from these perceived images until one sex endeavors to expand its prescribed role. This has largely been the case with women. They have been required to make the adjustments in both their appearance and body language in order to enter the professions and careers in our society that have long been associated with men. But men, too, have had to make adjustments, for they have been required to accept and to work with women who have broken the stereotyped image of what is feminine.

Women who are entering predominantly male vocations have been required to adapt their appearance and body language to the male paradigm. One reason for adopting the male mode of dress for a particular profession is that Americans have strong cultural expectations of their professional members of society. So intimately related are our expectations to the image of these professions, that the uniform or attire of a given profession alone is sufficient to invoke the appropriate or expected response to the profession itself.

If our responses are based on the assumption and tradition of men wearing white jackets with stethoscopes, or clad in blue with a gun, or attired in black robes with clerical collars, what happens when women, who have learned an entirely different repertoire of body language than their male counterparts, don these clothes — these professional symbols?

If women are to assume these types of positions in our culture, they, too, must learn to behave in a manner that will meet and expand the cultural expectations of society; they must both look and act the part of the professional role they are assuming. However, women can not, nor should they, physically abandon every gesture and mode of behavior they have learned over the years. In order to be effective, women who are entering traditionally male-dominated careers must find a mechanism for conveying the function of the profession through behavior that is both comfortable for women and appropriate for the position itself.

Clothes — the professional uniform — certainly form one means of demonstrating the outward function of a woman's professional role. We know that a woman in a blue uniform with a badge and a gun is a police officer. A woman in a con-servative suit at a law firm will most likely be regarded as an attorney. But the outward identification of a woman in a certain profession completes only part of the communication picture. *How* the woman communicates nonverbally affects whether or not she will be taken seriously in her role.

In Chapter II, we discussed studies which indicate that women usually contract within a given physical space, while men display more open and expansive body movements. We also considered how these distinct responses were interpreted. Female body language usually connotes accommodation and withdrawal while male kinesic behavior signals aggressive-ness and initiative.

If our culture so interprets such gestures, it is apparent that there are inherent conflicts for a woman who behaves in a stereotyped nonverbal female mode while attempting to perform a professional function that is closely associated with the customary male mode of behavior. There are ways for women to deal with this conflict. And they can do so without merely mimicking male nonverbal behavior patterns. Instead, women should be encouraged to combine their own nonverbal strengths with those typically male nonverbal patterns that can enhance professional as well as interpersonal communica-tion.

Some of the following distinctions in male-female nonverbal behavior were introduced in Chapter II. Men usually maintain direct eye contact when engaged in face-to-face conversation, while women often avert their eyes in the same situation. Women, who are encouraged to listen and not to interrupt others, demonstrate this by nodding their head more often than men during conversation, while men talk more and gesture less. An open body posture and movement is encouraged in men, while minimal and more polite gestures are considered proper behavior for women.

Women in positions of authority need to monitor their own body language. They should closely observe *how* others respond to them as well as how they react to others. In order for women to project a sense of assuredness, it is crucial to maintain an open and direct communication style.

It has been said that the eyes are the window to the soul. If this is so, it is important for women to sustain eye contact when speaking to others. It is equally crucial for women to sit and stand erect in order to project a forthright, rather than withdrawn image. Women's tendency to listen closely to others and to reflect this by nodding the head, demonstrates that communication contact has been made. This tendency serves women well. In fact, this type of response should be encouraged in men, for they are often accused of being disinterested or of not paying attention. Traditional male nonverbal communication suggests this perception. Effective masculine communication is diminished by a lack of gestures which reinforce the speaker's attempts at communication such as head nodding, sustained eye contact, and vocal affirmation (e.g., "Mmm hmm," "I see," "Yes," etc.). By strengthening their own positive nonverbal responses, and by borrowing those responses customarily reserved for the other sex, both men and women stand to expand their communication potential; to become better and more effective communicators.

SUMMARY

In this chapter on Professional Communication, we have explored both the verbal and nonverbal aspects of communicating effectively in a professional environment. Within professional settings, individuals use three communication modes: the one-to-one encounter; the group meeting; and the public communication forum. Each of these communication settings have requisite traits and techniques that can be mastered and improved upon in order to enhance communication between individuals. Women, who have long been regarded as less able than men in the professional arena, can utilize communication strategies to help present a stronger and more serious image than has been ascribed to them in the past.

In addition to the verbal professional image, the office environment has a language of its own, and how it is manipulated and controlled influences its effectiveness. How space and time are utilized communicates a great deal about the intentions and often the capabilities of an individual or of an organization. With careful consideration, and some forethought, improving nonverbal communication through the office environment can be achieved. Finally, our appearance — how we carry ourselves — signals a great deal about our own esteem as well as our competence in a particular role or function in society. Professionals from all sectors of society would do well to scrutinize what they, as individuals, communicate nonverbally to others, and how the profession in general is perceived.

It is important to emphasize that while different masculine and feminine communication styles exist, we are not advocating the use of one style over another. Both men and women need to be sensitive to what they are communicating as professionals and as individuals. They must consider the *intentions* of their communication encounters, considering whether they want to manipulate or control others, or whether they want to help and facilitate communication with others. If the latter is the case — which is in fact the more acceptable goal of *any* professional — then men and women must learn to share their communication strengths with each other *without* risk of being negatively stigmatized. *Only* through such genuine and total exchanges can truly effective communication be achieved.

SUGGESTED ACTIVITIES

A. Focus on Dyadic Communication: Nonverbal.

Try to recall the last time you visited an office for professional services, (e.g., physician, dentist, attorney, accountant, etc). Did you feel comfortable or uncomfortable? Using the following criteria, provide examples and analyze your responses:

1. Office environment
2. Attitude of office staff towards you
3. Waiting time to see the professional
4. Meeting with the professional
5. Attitude of the professional towards you

B. Focus on Dyadic Communication: Verbal/Nonverbal.

Have you ever met a person who was employed in an occupation uncharacteristic for their sex? (For example, a male nurse, a female police officer, a female minister, a male dental hygenist, a female neurosurgeon, etc.)

1. Using the nonverbal and verbal behavior of this individual as a basis, what was it about the individual's behavior that impressed you as either different or similar to your concept of the professional function this individual was performing?

2. After interacting with this individual for a period of time, did you become more accustomed to the person in his/her professional role? If yes, why? If no, why not?

C. Focus on Interpersonal Communication: Verbal/Nonverbal/ Listening.

1. Selecting the profession or career you are either pursuing or are currently in, how would you characterize:
   a) model verbal behavior
   b) model nonverbal behavior
   c) a model environment

2. Using the career or profession you selected above, what advice would you give to a member of the opposite sex about entering this profession on the subjects of:
   a) listening
   b) body language

D. Focus on Small Group Communication: Verbal/Nonverbal.

You have been asked to chair an important meeting for your firm. A week before the meeting, you learn that *all* of the members are of the opposite sex. What considerations and steps would you take to ensure a successful meeting?

E. Focus on Public Communication.

   1. Choose one side of one of the following topics:
    a) Pro-choice vs. anti-abortion
    b) Pro- vs. anti-gun control
    c) Pro- vs. anti-nuclear power
    d) Pro- vs. anti-smoking
    e) Pro- vs. capital punishment
    f) Pro- vs. anti-E.R.A.

You are invited to present a speech before an audience on one side of one of the above issues. How would you prepare the speech? What factors would you take into account prior to the engagement?

   2. Each student or seminar participant should deliver his/her speech to the rest of the group. The group should evaluate the speech using the following criteria:

   a) Does the speaker evidence a stereotypical verbal communication style for his/her gender?

   b) Does the speaker evidence a stereotypical nonverbal communication style for his/her gender?

   c) How would you rate the overall effectiveness of the speech? If the speech was particularly effective, what aspects contributed to its success? If the speech was not effective, in what areas were there deficiencies? What suggestions would you make for improvement?

F. Focus on Dyadic Communication.

   Arrange to interview at least two members of a certain profession making sure that both sexes are represented. Prepare a questionnaire dealing with some of the following topics:

    a) experiencing sexual harrassment
    b) being taken "seriously" by members of the same profession.
    c) reaction of others to the individuals' profession
    d) ability to advance within the profession
    e) perceived discrimination within the profession/firm/company.

Footnotes

[1] Erving Goffman's *Behavior in Public Places* and *The Presentation of Self in Everyday Life,* and H. Giles and P.F. Powesland's *Speech Style and Social Evaluation* explore responses to different segments of the population in American and British cultures.

[2] Barbara Westbrook Eakins and R. Gene Eakins, *Sex Differences in Human Communication,* (Boston: Houghton Mifflin Co., 1978), p. 166.

[3] A parallel study was done using the same written work — presumably one by a man; one by a woman. The work presumed to be written by a male was received and evaluated as more authoritative than the work ascribed to a woman author. It should be mentioned that similar experiments to verbal reception and perception have been conducted using minority children. The same speaker's voice was used to accompany a videotape of white, black and Mexican-American children. Viewers rated the intelligence of the three groups of children in the above order in spite of the fact that the voice was exactly the same. For further information in these experiements on minorities, consult Giles and Powesland, cited above.

[4] Edward T. Hall, *The Hidden Dimension,* (New York: Anchor Books, 1969), pps. 23-40.

[5] Deborah Borisoff, "The Image of the Dentist as the Product of the Practice," *The New York Journal of Dentistry,* 54:5, (Summer, 1984), p. 204.

[6] Ibid., p. 204.

[7] Linda L. Putnam, "Lady You're Trapped: Breaking out of Conflict Cycles," in *Women in Organizations: Barriers and Breakthroughs,* Ed. Joseph J. Pilotta, (Prospect Heights: Waveland Press, 1983), p. 48.

[8] It is important to bear in mind that we are discussing here scheduled meetings where the intention of the meeting is clear. Often, in the case of many agencies that are understaffed and that are designed to service whole segments of populations without specific appointments, waiting up to or more than one hour is not uncommon.

Chapter IV

MALE DOMINANCE AS A BARRIER TO CHANGE

May God be praised for woman
that gives up all her mind
A man may find in no man
A friendship of her kind
that covers all he has brought
As with her flesh and bone
Nor quarrels with a thought
Because it is not her own.
                    William Butler Yeats

According to Eleanor Holmes Norton in the Report of the New York City Commission on Human Rights:

> Much of the explanation for the entire range of...sex inequities ...can be easily summarized: job discrimination, continuing inequality in admissions to graduate, professional and technical schools, the stamp of "masculinity" on jobs ranging from banker to television repair man—jobs which require no "masculine" trait for performance, the unchanged attitudes of most men; and the still low level of awareness among women of their own problems.[1]

Although there have been decided changes since 1970 when the Commission first issued its report, many barriers to effective egalitarian communication between the sexes still exist. This chapter discusses barriers to change that are implicit in conventional attitudes about women's capabilities, their self-perceptions and how women are perceived by others. We will also discuss briefly legislation that has attempted to remove these obstacles.

I. ATTITUDES ABOUT WOMEN'S INHERENT
CAPABILITIES AS A BARRIER TO CHANGE

Traditionally, women in our society have been defined in terms of reproduction and nurturance; men in terms of protection and occupation. But the conventional white middle-class image of woman as wife, mother and full-time homemaker and of man as sole breadwinner belies the fact of most contemporary lives. Women are no longer peripheral members of the work force. At present, 52% of all females in America are working outside the home.[2] Hence, traditional attitudes about women's natural capabilities may form obstacles not only to their achievement, but to their very survival. These attitudes fall into two basic categories; the belief either that 1) women are not inherently *able* to perform tasks as well as men, or that 2) even when able, women *should not* compete with men in the work place.

The assumption exists that half the human race is constitutionally more fit for work that requires the ability to nurture and serve rather than to plan and initiate. This stereotype has been used to exclude each sex from occupations that are traditionally associated with the other.

Thus, women have frequently been tracked into dead-end, "entry-level" jobs in numerous fields, while males with similar degrees of experience and expertise have been hired on more upwardly mobile tracts. The female college graduate is still more likely to be expected to break into a field as a typist or receptionist than is her male counterpart. *Women's conventional communication strengths have been used against them,* as an excuse for hiring women and keeping them in positions where they are expected to smile, greet and serve others. Males with identical degrees are more likely to be employed in positions where they may learn aspects of a business and proceed through its ranks. The efficient secretary may be promoted to executive secretary, while the beginning salesman whose achievements are recognized may hope to be promoted to a managerial position. Although it is not impossible for women to bypass either clerical channels or to ascend to more substantial positions within an organization, they still have to overcome the burden of traditional sex role expectations.

In recent years, higher and professional education has become available to larger numbers of women. Moreover, it has become socially acceptable for women to pursue an education, and it is more likely to be financially feasible for many to do so. However, women still dominate the helping professions, (e.g., nursing, elementary school teaching, dental hygiene, etc.), and men still dominate those professional specialties, (e.g., medicine, college teaching, dentistry, etc.), regarded as more prestigious. Thus, overcoming the "stamp of masculinity" is an issue for women in many occupations. Most often the stock broker, the real estate salesperson and the physician are males. Women who have broken into these fields are still clustered in relatively less lucrative, less prestigious, and less conventionally masculine specialties.

Women's traditional skills in and associations with the home and the family affect others' perceptions of their abilities. For example, women in real estate are more often employed in residential than in corporate sales. A much larger percentage of female physicians are pediatricians rather than surgeons. In Jill Quadrango's article assessing medical specialties, she found that many female physicians indicated that their choice of a specialty was influenced by their desire to avoid possible conflicts which they feared might arise if they entered more traditionally male areas.[3]

Even among those who do not assert that women's inherent capabilities are less or different than men's, there are those who believe that women *should not* enter careers that are labelled as traditionally male. Some argue that women don't really "need" to work, and that, when they do, they may be taking a job away from a male who is responsible for the support of an entire family. However, commissioner Eleanor Holmes Norton set this assumption to rest when she stated that:

> Eight million women heads of families need to join the struggle for women's rights, to take to task that large segment of the population who believe women work for pin money. So do the 84% of mothers who, though living with their husbands, must work to supplement low male wages; so do the one third of working mothers who go to work though they have children under six years of age and no adequate child care facilities.[4]

Overwhelmingly, women, like men, work because they must; because they are solely or partially responsible for their own and their family's sustenance. Yet many still assume that, regardless of individual skills and proclivities, females should conduct themselves in a stereotypical manner, functioning basically in a supportive capacity and eschewing occupations which demand more assertive communication styles.

At home, working women are still considered to be more responsible for childcare and domestic chores than are their male partners. Hence, women are discouraged from pursuing occupations that demand a considerable commitment of an individual's time and energies. Employers may fear that women will be less responsible to their careers because of their great responsibilities to their families.

However, women who do not have familial constraints are also restricted in the workplace. Some prospective employers and colleagues regard unmarried women with suspicion. They may speculate that the woman is merely looking for a husband and will leave or lessen her commitment to her career should she marry. Furthermore, women who do not communicate in a stereotypical feminine mode reflecting indecision, uncertainty or the need for male approval, may threaten men who are un-accustomed to dealing with independent women who appear not to need them.

II. SELF-PERCEPTIONS AS A BARRIER TO CHANGE

In addition to how they are perceived by others, men and women's perceptions of themselves may present significant ob-stacles. Many women have internalized societal values that place a high premium on traits that are conventionally identi-fied as masculine, and ascribe low status to feminine qualities. Women may communicate this negative self-perception in several ways.

1. Women may attempt to disassociate themselves from other women, and so distance themselves from males' devalua-tion of them. As Stockard and Johnson observe:

> One possible response to devaluation is for women to see it as correct on a general level but to insist that "it doesn't apply to

me because I'm not like other women." Thus, women who have
made it in a man's world often attribute their success to their
being better than and fundamentally different from other
women. Isolated professional women may feel, "I made it. Why
can't the rest of you?"[5]

By accepting that they are special, unique or unlike other
women, females may be participating in their own self-deni-
gration and confirming negative stereotypes.

2. Women may fear that their own success will lead others
to regard them as less feminine. Matina Horner measured
achievement motivation of college students. Undergraduates
were asked to complete a story based on the sentence, "After
first-term finals, John(Anne) finds himself(herself) at the top of
his (her) medical school class." Over 65% of the females, but
under 10% of the males indicated concern about doing well. In
their stories about "Anne," female students expressed fears of
social rejection as a result of success.[6]

While men are expected to succeed in the workplace, and in
fact are encouraged to measure their self-worth in terms of
what they have accomplished in the public sphere, a significant proportion of women anticipate that their success will be
resented. Thus women who experience *fear* of success are not
concerned that they are less capable than men. Rather, the
barrier is a result of an awareness that the more capable they
are, the more likely they are to be treated negatively. Andrea
Dworkin contends that women learn fear as a function of femininity, and that the fear women experience is isolating,
confusing and debilitating.[7] Women fear if they act in an unfeminine manner, they will be isolated, avoided and ignored.
Furthermore, women are confused because they are frequently
chastised or punished for the very behaviors for which males
are rewarded — for speaking loudly and forcefully, for example. Finally, this fear is incremental. Each time a woman vio-
lates sex-role stereotyped expectations, she is subject to such
negative treatment that she learns to anticipate the sanctions
against her, and so she restricts herself. The tenacity with
which both men and women adhere to prescribed behavior
patterns and role expectations may therefore reflect their fear
of the consequences that change would engender. The fear of
change has implications for women and men in personal as
well as in occupational settings.

III. BARRIERS TO CHANGE IN THE HOMEFRONT

Earlier, we mentioned that often men have been raised with the understanding that their ability to provide security for a family was a measure of their manhood. Their sights, therefore, were set on the workplace. In the past, women have been led to believe that womanhood was equated primarily with being a devoted wife and mother. Their sights, therefore, were set on the home environment; on the family. However, the changing roles of women in society have had an enormous effect on the concept of home and family and on the ability to form and sustain the open communication that is requisite in any relationship.

Most of the communication breakdowns that occur between partners result from a lack of understanding. There are three major problem areas where change may disrupt a relationship. They are: control of money, designation of responsibilities, and participation in childcare.

1. *The Working Woman and Money.*

Based on the data collected from 12,000 questionnaires, sociologists Blumstein and Schwartz report, "Most men cannot understand how working might be considered a privilege. From the time they are little boys, they know they are *expected* to have a job, perhaps a career — at the very least, to make a living for themselves."[8]

For the majority of men, their manhood and their self-esteem are intimately tied to professional achievements. Further, the role of *provider*, of safeguarding and protecting the family is a natural consequence of succeeding at work. When women and men conform to and believe in the traditional roles of the family, the *status quo* is maintained and the culturally prescribed role of the married couple remains in tact.

However, when one partner attempts to *change* his or her prescribed role, the relationship may be threatened. Men may fear a potential loss of status when their partners work. A large part of a man's self-esteem results from the professional position or rank he holds in the workplace. A husband who sees his wife rising in her own career may often compare achievement and view her success as his failure. How couples deal with change will affect the success of a relationship. In the area of earning money, women have indeed challenged the traditional image of the male as sole provider. Because many men have been conditioned to equate their own success with the amount of money they earn, men's power in the relationship is affected when the capacity to earn more than their partner is threatened.

It is therefore understandable why many husbands are resistent to their partner's career. Rather than trying to prevent the spouse from working, those threatened would benefit by understanding the following:

a) The majority of women in America work because they have to contribute to the family's income. Instead of construing such need as competition, or as a sleight to one's manhood, men should regard their spouse's contribution to the household as alleviating them from the burden of providing total economic support.

b) Most women who work do not do so to wield power over the family. Working women usually derive a sense of equality, (not superiority), and respectability, (not control), from their careers.

c) Those couples who *share* the control and decision-making over monetary matters, are more likely to have a relationship that is based upon mutual sharing and trust.

2. *The Working Woman and the Designation of Responsibil- in the Home.*

Monetary control is not the only area that can undermine the traditional power dynamics of a relationship. There are other concerns that deal with the relationship *itself* when both partners are employed. These concerns include: the amount of time and emotional support expected by each partner, and the allocation of tasks.

a) Time and emotional support.

Blumstein and Schwartz differentiate between "work-centered" and "relationship-centered" individuals and couples.[9] Men have been encouraged to focus their efforts on their jobs and careers. Traditionally, women have been expected to devote themselves to their home and family, and to reflect their own success through their husband's accomplishments. In such a traditional household, the less work-centered partner is expected to derive emotional satisfaction from spending time with the other partner: taking care of her/him; being taken care of by another.

However, when both partners spend an equal amount of time at work, the energy and amount of time that the traditional wife might have devoted to meeting her *husband's* needs, is considerably diminished. Ideally, each partner must contribute to the relationship. A relationship that is not carefully attended to can not sustain itself. Both partners need to express their needs openly and honestly and discuss strategies to meet them. Both must allow for time to spend privately with each other and must share the responsibility for making sure that the relationship does not become weakened.

Many couples spend a great deal of energy complaining about the lack of time they have with each other. Such efforts can be put to more efficient use by channeling these complaints into a constructive dialogue.

b) Allocation of tasks.

"...new marriages are more likely to fail when the husband feels his wife does not do her fair share of the household tasks." according to Blumstein and Schwartz.[10] Making sure that the home is maintained, the clothes cleaned, and the dinner prepared has been and continues to be primarily the responsibility of women. So strongly are these duties associated with women in relationships that men at times use cleaning the house as an excuse to prevent their spouses from seeking employment. In one of the interviews conducted by Blumstein and Schwartz, a 48-year-old male plastic surgeon provides a typical response:

> I don't mind her having a part-time job, but she doesn't have time for a full-time job....I am the breadwinner, she is the home-maker, and that is what we signed up for twenty years ago....I don't mind her working as long as dinner is ready on time and the house is neat and clean.[11]

In informal interviews we have conducted, other men and women confide that the men will "help out" around the house as long as no one else knows about it. Many men still equate doing household chores with stereotyped feminine behavior and performing such tasks themselves may be construed by others as diminishing their own masculinity. A more equitable division of tasks is necessary if both parties are to feel that their respective contributions to the relationship are of equal value.

3. *The Working Woman and the Family.*

The working female parent must often deal with a great deal of pressure when trying to cope with both raising a child and pursuing a career. These pressures exist at the workplace and home. In both instances, the result of confronting resistance is to debilitate and to weaken her efforts to be a competent parent and professional.

Guilt is a powerful force and working parents are susceptible to criticism about how well their children are being cared for. Often criticism appears at home in the form of husbands expecting their wives to be fully responsible for child-care. One myth that has been perpetuated as a reason to keep women at home is that women make better parents because they know how to nurture and men do not. As early as 1935, Margaret Mead in *Sex and Temperament in Three Primitive Societies* refuted the notion that nurturant behavior was the exclusive domain of women.[12] She presented other cultures where male members demonstrated nurturing behavior. Subsequent research has supported Mead's thesis, and male nurturing behavior as one means of bonding parent to child is encouraged as an important aspect of participating in the experience of being a parent.

When "being a better parent" is not the issue, husbands sometimes invoke their conventional perogative as head of the household to require their wives to do everything. Such statements as, "I don't mind her working just so long as I don't have to clean up after the kids," is an example of the type of justification that puts the onus on the woman to assume total responsibility at home. This type of response further sets up the "super-mom" syndrome of having to do absolutely everything well and to carry the burden of two full-time jobs.

Often, the most powerful barrier in the home is a woman's *own* sense that she can not balance her two roles — especially when she has children. The fear of leaving her children in someone else's care is potent enough to prevent her from venturing outside the home, or to stigmatize her when she must work outside the home.

These attitudes restrict men as well as women by placing them in a stereotyped mode from which it is difficult to break out. Fortunately, within the past several decades, the social pressures urging *all* individuals to pursue their vocational aspirations and to participate more fully in responsibilities at home have begun to liberate both sexes from prescribed roles. While the barriers still exist, they are becoming less powerful. It would be an ideal world if we could attribute all of the social changes and progress in the status of women in society today to an evolutionary process. This, unfortunately, is not the case. But the social stirrings of the past have certainly *facilitated* and encouraged political pressure. As a result, laws have been enacted that are intended to protect and safeguard the rights of women and minorities to education and to equal opportunities in the workplace.

IV. THE WORKING WOMAN AND THE LAW

Since 1963, four laws have been enacted to ensure the legal status of women (and also minorities). The Equal Pay Act of 1963 was introduced to guarantee "equal pay for equal work." Those organizations who do not comply with this regulation risk incurring liability for not paying equal wages, and may be required to pay back wages to those who have been discriminated against.

The second major law levelled against discrimination at the workplace was Title VII of the Civil Rights Act of 1964. This law was established to assure fair and equal employment practices of all people regardless of sex, race, religion and national origin.

The Executive Order 11375 of 1967 was established to guarantee that those employers contracting with the federal government would be prohibited from sex discrimination acts or would risk the termination of existing contracts.

The fourth and most recent law is Title IX of the Education Amendments of 1972 which guarantees equal protection to all individuals who are participating in any educational program or activity in an organization or institution receiving Federal financial assistance. Violating this law can also result in the termination of aid.

In his article, "Women in Organizations: The Impact of Law," Lawrence Baum exposes the limitations of these laws.[13] The potential impact of the above legislation has been affected by both the lack of adequate enforcement, and by the potential plaintiff's fear of reprisal.

1. Ability to Enforce the Law.

The assurance that any law is adhered to and that any infraction is swiftly responded to are the responsibilities of many agencies. However, if adequate funding, staffing, commitment and priorities are lacking, the efficiency and effectiveness of an agency will be considerably weakened. This has been a problem for many of the agencies trying to enforce these laws and to pursue claims levelled against organizations.

2. Reluctance to File a Suit.

A second reason for the laws' limited power is the reluctance of the plaintiff to file a suit. There are many reasons why a woman (or any individual being discriminated against) would refrain from starting a suit. One major reason is the financial burden and potential time engendered with a lawsuit. A less overt, but not less powerful, consideration is the fear of subtle and overt retaliatory actions that one might receive while in the midst of litigation.

In spite of these limitations, the potential good and positive future implications for protecting women under the law cannot be overlooked. Baum concludes his article with the following statement:

> I have given some emphasis to the limits of the law as a force against discrimination, because those limits often are overlooked. But it also is important to keep in mind the significance of what has happened to the law in the past two decades. For most of our history the law accepted and even encouraged discrimination against women. Now we have laws that explicitly prohibit discrimination. Whatever effect these laws have, they have put government in the position of proclaiming support for equality rather than for inequality. That in itself is a revolutionary change.[14]

SUMMARY

In this chapter, we have explained how the *desire* to pursue a goal may not be sufficient to enable one to reach it. This is true for both women and men. However, in the area of choice of careers and of success in a position, there are barriers to achievement for women for reasons *other* than ability.

Three kinds of barriers to professional mobility predominate. First, a belief in a lack of *innate* ability to *perform* certain tasks is one rationale used to keep women from entering or advancing in certain jobs, and for staying in other positions that are lowpaying and do not allow for upward mobility.

Second, social stereotypes of communicative behavior are used to justify why women *should* or *should not* pursue certain positions. In this instance, issues of gender role in society rather than capability is employed to maintain the *status quo* in education and business.

The third barrier to change, and the most potent indeed, is one's self-perception. Individuals who fear violating the traditional norms for masculine and feminine behavior have a great deal of difficulty overcoming the labels and effectuating change.

One's personal relationship may present a fourth barrier to change. Men and women who have grown accustomed to a certain lifestyle and relationship pattern which reinforce their prescribed roles, are not going to relinquish these patterns easily to embrace what is unknown.

SUGGESTED ACTIVITIES

All of the following exercises focus on dyadic, interpersonal communication.

1. The following comments were taken from Blumstein and Schwartz' book, *American Couples.* Use each comment as a basis for discussion, using the following opening statement as a starting point:

"This statement may be a barrier to communication because..." (Depending upon the nature of the statement, relate your answer to barriers to communication, using how men and women are perceived, how they perceive themselves, and the barriers that may exist or arise within the home.)

a) husband, age 26

"She kids me sometimes, like why don't I stay home and be a house-husband and she'll go out and take over. But she just does that to rile me. She knows I would never allow that and I know she wouldn't like it if I said that would be great. ...It's hard to imagine a man who would feel good living off a woman." (pp. 71-72)

b) husband, age 39:

"I have always thought that I would be the primary bread-winner and even though I don't have to be, I can't get over the idea that I should be....I am used to having everyone rely on me....I don't want to feel dependent....It's not really masculine....When I see myself as less masculine, I see her as more self-sufficient and more masculine, which isn't so great.... It affects my sexual interest and the way I feel about the relationship." (p. 73)

c) wife, age 37:

"He didn't mind me helping out with political campaigns, but when I started to have a real career—(the arguments started). For my part, I am enjoying what I am doing and I think I am getting better at it. I also think I'm more interesting because of it and I think he should feel that way too....I think he is threatened at our relationship changing and I try and reassure him that things will just get better. I think I'm a much nicer, happier person these days, and I just have to show him that in terms he can see and not get defensive about." (p. 121)

d) wife, age 41:

"He's been very supportive too. I was a little worried about that, but he's been great. He's very proud of me (working...)" (p. 122)

e) husband, age 35:

"She thinks I am being very unreasonable about the limits I put on her work. But you have to see this in the context of the life we have made together. We have worked out things very well by her staying at home and raising our children and me bringing home the bacon. I find it odd now that she wants to go out and do somebody else's dirty work when she could stay at home and use the life we worked hard to put together. We argue about this about once a month, especially when she is grouchy because of something someone in the office said or did. I'll tell her again to quit and let me provide and she'll get huffy and unreasonable." (p. 133)

f) wife, late 20's: "He has me on this pedestal — maybe I should say he needs to have me on this pedestal — where I am his wife and mother of his children and that's what I am. I don't need all of this. I would like to get out and do a little work and add a little to our bank account so we can travel. He gets quiet and angry when I try and discuss why this would be a benefit, and sometimes he just gets up and walks away. I think he thinks I am saying something about him, but I try and tell him I am only saying something about me and what I would like." (p. 133)

2. The class or seminar group should be divided into mixed-sex pairs. Assuming that each couple are married parents who work and earn approximately the same amount of money, the couples should negotiate the delegation of responsibilities and report on the following:

a) How much time do you allocate to taking care of your children?

b) How much time and what type of tasks do you perform in the home?

c) Prepare a chart that depicts a typical work week (Monday through Friday), and how you have assigned and shared duties related to the home, and duties related to the children.

3. The class or seminar group should be divided into mixed-sex pairs. The pairs should be further designated into the following four separate categories:

a) Men interview women demonstrating a strong stereotyped bias about a woman's capability to perform the job;

b) Women interview men demonstrating a strong stereotyped bias about a man's capability to perform the job;

c) Men interview women demonstrating the absence of stereotyped values; and

   d) Women interview men demonstrating the absence of stereotyped values.

The above groups will simulate an interview for a position in management. The position description is as follows:

"Dynamic individual with strong administrative and management skills needed for high-pressured position in a major corporation. Excellent communication skills a must. This high visibility position includes entertaining clients, and some travelling. Room for advancement for the right person. Salary negotiable."

The rest of the group should evaluate the interviews using the following criteria:

   a) Monitor the types of questions asked by the interviewer and interviewee under each of the four categories designated above;
   b) Compare the nonverbal and verbal behavior among the four groups; and
   c) Examine and evaluate the speaker-listener relationship among the four groups.

Footnotes

[1] Eleanor Holmes Norton, introduction, *Women's Role in Contemporary Society: The Report of the New York City Commission on Human Rights*, September 21-25, 1970, (New York: Avon Books, 1972), p. 27.

[2] U.S. Bureau of the Census, *Current Population Reports* series P-20, (1981, 1982) and series P-23 (1981, 1982).

[3] Jill Quadrango, "Occupational Sex-Typing and Internal Labor Market Distributions: An Assessment of Medical Specialties," *Social Problems*, 23 (1976), 442-53.

[4] Norton, "A Strategy for Change" in *Women's Role in Contemporary Society*, p. 59.

[5] Jean Stockard and Miriam M. Johnson, *Sex Roles: Sex Inequality and Sex Role Development*, (Englewood Cliffs, N.J.: Prentice-Hall, Inc., 1980), p. 16.

[6] Matina Horner, "Toward an Understanding of Achievement-related Conflicts in Women," *Journal of Social Issues*, 28 (1972), 157-175.

[7] Andrea Dworkin, "The Sexual Politics of Fear and Courage," in *Our Blood: Prophesies and Discourses on Sexual Politics*, (New York: Perigee Books, G.P. Putnam's Sons, 1976), p. 59.

[8] Philip Blumstein and Pepper Schwartz, *American Couples: Money, Work, Sex*, (New York: William Morrow and Co., Inc., 1983), p. 117.

[9]Ibid., p. 165.

[10]Ibid., p. 312.

[11]Ibid., p. 118.

[12]Margaret Mead, *Sex and Temperament in Three Primitive Societies,* (New York: Morrow, 1963).

[13]Lawrence Baum, "Women in Organizations: The Impact of Law," in *Women in Organizations: Barriers and Breakthroughs,* ed. Joseph J. Pilotta, (Prospect Heights, Ill.: Waveland Press, Inc. 1983), pp. 55-71.

[14]Ibid., pp. 70-71.

Chapter V — Conclusion

EFFECTING CHANGE
Expanding Human Potential

No matter what women and men *consciously* say or do, part of every message which they send and which others receive expresses their self-perception and their sense of relative power. How one speaks, moves or listens tells us how that person sees her- or himself. An individual cannot *not* communicate. (For example, the choice to be silent tells us as much about a person as the choice to speak.) And so, gender-based stereotypes are manifested through communicative behaviors.

However, in the field of speech communication, gender is a variable that has only recently been addressed. Although there is no aspect of the discipline in which gender is not a factor, relatively few texts deal with the ramifications of these differences. Yet, for the prospective therapist or counselor, a study of dyadic communication and interview techniques is incomplete unless one is cognizant of the potential impact of gender differences upon the interview. Similarly, the business person who studies group dynamics needs to be apprised of the possible effects of differing sex-role expectations in the workplace. The hierarchies of small groups, leadership and role taking functions, are all affected by these differences. Future public speakers in law, politics, education or any other field, need to be aware of how their gender may facilitate or impede the reception of their message. The bilingual student and the future teacher of nonnative English speakers must learn to distinguish those linguistic and paralinguistic constructs that are based on specifically male/female usage from those that are not. And all of us, in the most intimate of the interpersonal relationships in our lives, will only be able to share openly and honestly with each other if we are sensitive to the potential power imbalances between us that may be exacerbated by gender-linked communication differences.

In this book, we have introduced you to these differences and discussed their impact in professional settings. While it would be impossible to address adequately every possible aspect of communication in a book of this scope, we have tried to present you with representative examples of contexts in which gender differences affect communication. We have maintained throughout that, although the traditional male mode of behavior has been generally considered stronger and more effective, neither masculine nor feminine communicative acts are *inherently* better or worse; stronger or weaker. Rather, it is the *interpretation* that has been placed upon these respective styles that has led people to value one over the other; to reward certain behaviors and punish others. It is that interpretation that we call into question.

The very existence of this book is evidence of the fact that the world is changing. At the National Democratic Convention in July, 1984, Governor Mario Cuomo of New York asserted that his party spoke for "reasonable people who are fighting to preserve our very existence from a macho intransigence" on the part of politicians who refuse to responsibly discuss the possibilities and dangers of nuclear war.[1] By ascribing the threat of nuclear holocaust to a "macho intransigence," Cuomo was equating global militarism with a specifically male model of aggression. To be intransigent is to be unwilling or unable to compromise, to reconcile or to come to an agreement. The stereotypical masculine communicative behaviors such as categorical assertions, interruptions and commands foster intransigent attitudes.

As we have seen in the previous chapter, there is still a pressing need to overcome the barrier of male dominance in the workplace, in the home, and in the law. Similarly, we need to overcome the fears and negative self-perceptions of those who are less powerful as a result of others' dominance. Instead of perpetuating male and female styles as polar opposites, we have suggested ways that women and men might use effectively the strategies conventionally associated with the opposite sex. In order for these strategies to be adopted, we must remove depreciatory associations for female behavior by expanding traditional views of strength and weakness.

The stereotypically feminine style of discourse is less direct and assertive than the masculine, and more desirous of affirmation and approval. However, it is only when we look at the conventional feminine behavior through a masculine bias that women's strategies appear "weak" or "passive." Psychologist Carol Gilligan has explained that "When the focus on...individual achievement...is equated with personal autonomy, concern with relationships appear as a weakness of women rather than as a human strength."[2] Without the accustomed bias, traditional feminine behaviors may be interpreted as manifestations of a deeper human strength. As poet Adrienne Rich has affirmed:

> ...gentleness is active
> gentleness swabs at the crusted stump
>
> invents more merciful instruments
> to touch the wound beyond the wound
>
> does not faint with disgust
> will not be driven off
>
> keeps bearing witness calmly
> against the predator, the parasite.[3]

We would hope that both men and women might learn, in Rich's words, to value and to employ "more merciful instruments" when communicating with others. Patricia Hayes Bradley found in her research on the use of tag questions and qualifying statements by both men and women, that while these stereotypically feminine linguistic devices "were perceived as indicators of uncertainty and nonassertiveness when used by women...males were able to use them with virtual impunity." In fact, the "feminine" strategies were perceived as "tools of politeness and other-directedness when employed by men."[4]

Likewise, women who incorporate into their communicative style some of the direct masculine modes are often more able to effectuate their needs than are more traditional women.

Thus, we advocate for both sexes an androgynous model, in

which traditional masculine and feminine traits are blended. As Sandra Bem and Darryl J. Bem state:

> Men and women are no longer to be stereotyped by society's definitions. If sensitivity, emotionality and warmth are desirable human characteristics, then they are desirable for men as well as for women....If independence, assertiveness and serious intellectual commitment are desirable human characteristics, then they are desirable for women as well as for men. The major prescription of this college generation is that each individual should be encouraged to discover and fulfill his/her own unique potential and identity, unfettered by society's presumptions.[5]

While we echo Bem and Bem's sentiment, we realize that male and female behavior cannot fully evolve in an androgynous direction until the social institutions that place value on one mode over another are changed. But we can begin by looking at, by listening to and questioning the conventions that have been embraced by both sexes for so long. Only then will we be able to reach out and understand each other.

Footnotes

[1]"Transcript of Keynote Address by Cuomo to the Convention," *New York Times*, July 17, 1984, p. A16.

[2]Carol Gilligan, *In a Different Voice: Psychological Theory and Women's Development*, (Cambridge, Mass.: Harvard University Press, 1982), p. 17.

[3]Adrienne Rich, "Natural Resources," in *The Dream of a Common Language, Poems 1974-1977*, (New York: W.W. Norton, & Co., 1978), pp. 63-64.

[4]Patricia Hayes Bradley, "The Folk-Linguistics of Women's Speech: An Empirical Examination," *Communication Monographs*, 48 (March 1981), 90.

[5]Sandra Bem and Darryl J. Bem, "Training the Woman to Know Her Place: The Power of a Nonconscious Ideology," in *Women's Role in Contemporary Society*, p. 104.

BIBILOGRAPHY

Argyle, Michael, Lalljee, Mansur and Cook, Mark. "The Effects of Visibility on Interaction in a Dyad." *Human Relations*. 21 (1968): 3-17.

Austin, William. "Some Social Aspects of Paralanguage." *Canadian Journal of Linguistics*. 11 (1965): 31-39.

Berkin, Carol Ruth and Norton, Mary Beth, Eds. *Women in America: A History*. Boston: Houghton Mifflin Co., 1979.

Blumstein, Philip, and Schwartz, Pepper. *American Couples: Money, Work, Sex*. New York: William Morrow & Co., Inc., 1983.

Borisoff, Deborah. "The Image of the Dentis as the Product of the Practice." *The New York Journal of Dentistry*. 54 (July-July-August, 1984): 203-206.

Brend, Ruth. "Male-Female Intonation Patterns in American English." In Barrie Thorne and Nancy M. Henley, Eds. *Language and Sex: Difference and Dominance*. Rowley, Mass.: Newbury House, 1975.

de Beauvoir, Simone. *The Second Sex*. Trans. and Ed., H.M. Parshley. New York: Bantam Books, Alfred A. Knopf, Inc., 1952.

Duberman, Lucille. *Gender and Sex in Society*. New York: Praeger Publishers, Inc., 1975.

Dworkin, Andrea. *Our Blood: Prophesies and Discourses on Sexual Politics*. New York: Perigee Books, G.P. Putnam's Sons, 1976.

Eakins, Barbara Westbrook and Eakins, R. Gene. *Sex Differences in Human Communication*. Boston: Houghton Mifflin Co., 1978.

Ellsworth, Phoebe C., Carlsmith, J. Merrill, and Henson, A. "The Stare as a Stimulus to Flight in Human Subjects: A Series of Field Experiments." *Journal of Personality and Social Psychology*. 21 (1972): 302-11.

Exline, Ralph, Gray, David, and Shuette, Dorothy. "Visual Behavior in a Dyad as Affected by Interview Content and Sex of Respondent." *Journal of Personality and Social Psychology*. 1 (1965): 207-09.

Flexner, Eleanor. *Century of Struggle: The Woman's Rights Movement in the United States*. New York: Atheneum, 1968.

Giles, H. and Powesland, P.F. *Speech Style and Social Evaluation.* London: Academic Press, 1975.

Gilligan, Carol. *In a Different Voice: Psychological Theory and Women's Development.* Cambridge, Mass.: Harvard University Press, 1982.

Goffman, Erving. *The Presentation of Self in Everyday Life.* Garden City, N.Y.: Anchor Doubleday Books, 1959.

_____. *Behavior in Public Places.* New York: The Free Press, 1963.

Hall, Edward T. *The Hidden Dimension.* Garden City, N.Y.: Anchor Books, 1969.

_____. *The Silent Language.* Garden City, N.Y.: Anchor Books, 1973.

Henley, Nancy M. *Body Politics: Power, Sex and Non Verbal Communication.* Englewood Cliffs, N.J.: Prentice-Hall, 1977.

Hochschild, Arlie Russell. "Smile Wars: Counting the Casualties of Emotional Labor." *Mother Jones.* (December, 1983): 35-42.

Horner, Matina. "Toward and Understanding of Achievement Related Conflicts in Women." *Journal of Social Issues.* 28 (1972): 157-75.

Keller, Evelyn Fox. "Feminism as an Analytic Tool for the Study of Science." *Academe.* Bulletin of the American Association of University Professors. (September-October, 1983)..

Keohane, Nanherl O. "Speaking from Silence: Women and the Science of Politics." In *A Feminist Perspective in the Academy.* Eds. Elizabeth Langland and Walter Gove. Chicago: University of Chicago Press, 1981.

Kramarae, Chris. *Women and Men Speaking: Frameworks for Analysis.* Rowley, Mass.: Newbury House, 1981.

Labov, William. *Sociolinguistic Patterns.* Philadelphia: University of Pennsylvania Press, 1972.

Lakoff, Robin. *Language and Woman's Place.* New York: Harper and Row, 1975.

Larkin, Joan. *Housework.* Brooklyn, New York: Out and Out Books, 1975.

Martin, Wendy, Ed. *American Sisterhood: Writings of the Feminist Movement from Colonial Times to the Present.* New York: Harper and Row, Inc., 1972.

Mattingly, Ignatius. "Speaker Variation and Vocal Tract Size." Paper presented at the Acoustical Society of America, 1966. Abstract in *Journal of Acoustical Society of America* 39 (1966): 1219.

Mead, Margaret. *Sex and Temperament in Three Primitive Societies.* New York: Morrow, 1963.

Merrill, Lisa. "Communicative Strategies of Women in Dentistry." *The New York Journal of Dentistry.* 54 (June-July-August 1984): 207-210.

Nierenberg, Gerald I. and Calero, Henry H. *How to Read a Person Like a Book*. New York: Hawthorne, 1971; Pocket Books, 1973.

Nilsen, Alleen Pace; Bosmajian, Haig; Gershuny, H. Lee, and Stanley, Julia P. *Sexism and Language*. Urbana, Illinois: National Council of Teachers of English, 1977.

Norton, Eleanor Holmes, Introduction. *Women's Role in Contemporary Society*. The Report of the New York City Commission on Human Rights, September 21-25, 1970. New York: Avon Books, 1972.

Pilotta, Joseph L., Ed. *Women in Organizations: Barriers and Breakthroughs*. Prospect Heights, Illinois: Waveland Press, Inc., 1983.

Quadrango, Jill. "Occupational Sex-Typing and Internal Labor Market Distributions: An Assessment of Medical Specialties." *Social Problems* 23 (1976): 442-53.

Rich, Adrienne. *On Lies, Secrets and Silence: Selected Prose 1966-1978*. New York: W.W. Norton and Co., 1979.

_____. *The Dream of a Common Language, Poems 1974-1977*. New York: W.W. Norton and Co., 1978.

Ruether, Rosemary. "Feminist Critique in Religious Studies." In *A Feminist Perspective in the Academy*. Eds. Elizabeth Langland and Walter Gove. Chicago: University of Chicago Press, 1981.

Ryan, Mary P. *Womanhood in America*. New York: Franklin Watts, 1975.

Sachs, Jacqueline; Liberman, Philip and Erickson, Donna. "Anatomical and Cultural Determinants of Male and Female Speech." In *Language Attitudes: Current Trends and Prospects*. Eds. Roger W. Shuy and Ralph W. Fasold. Washington, D.C.: Georgetown University Press, 1973.

Scheflen, Albert E. *Body Language and Social Order: Communication as Behavioral Control*. Englewood Cliffs, New Jersey: Prentice-Hall, 1972.

Shuy, Roger W.; Wolfram, Walter A. and Riley, William K. *Linguistic Correlates of Social Stratification in Detroit Speech*. Final Report, Project 6-1347. Washington, D.C.: Office of Education, 1967.

Sieburg, Evelyn and Larson, Carl. "Dimensions of Interpersonal Response." Paper presented to the Internal Communication Association. Phoenix, Arizona, 1971.

Silveira, Jeanette. "Thoughts on the Politics of Touch." *Women's Press*, (Eugene, Oregon) 1, (February, 1972): 13.

Steil, Lyman K.; Barker, Larry L. and Watson, Kittie W. *Effective Listening: Key to Your Success*. Reading, Massachusetts: Addison-Wesley, 1983.

Steinem, Gloria. *Outrageous Acts and Everyday Rebellions*. New York: Holt, Rinehart, Winston, 1983.

Stockard, Jean and Johnson, Miriam M. *Sex roles: Sex Inequality and Sex Role Development.* Englewood Cliffs, New Jersey: Prentice-Hall, Inc., 1980.

Stone, Janet and Bachner, Jane. *Speaking Up: A Book for Every Woman Who Wants to Speak Effectively.* New York: McGraw Hill Book Co., 1977.

Strodtbeck, Fred; James, Rita M., and Hawkins, Charles. "Social Status in Jury Deliberations." *American Sociological Review* 22 (1957): 718.

————. and Mann, Richard D. "Sex Role Differentiation in Jury Deliberations." *Sociometry* 19 (1956): 3-11.

Thorne, Barrie and Henley, Nancy M., Eds. *Language and Sex: Difference and Dominance.* Rowley, Massachusetts: Newbury House, 1975.

Trudgill, Peter. "Sex, Covert Prestige and Linguistic Change in the Urban British English of Norwich." In *Language and Sex: Difference and Dominance.* Barrie Thorne and Nancy M. Henley, Eds. Rowley, Massachusetts: Newbury House, 1975.

Uris, Dorothy. *A Woman's Voice: A Handbook to Successful Private and Public Speaking.* New York: Barnes and Noble Books; Harper and Row, 1975.

Willis, Frank. "Initial Speaking Distance as a Function of the Speaker's Relationship." *Psychonomic Science* 5 (1966): 221-22.

Wilson, Paul R. "Perceptual Distortion of Height as a Function of Ascribed Academic Status." *Journal of Social Psychology* 74 (1968): 97-102.

Wolff, Florence I.; Marsnik, Nadine C.; Tracey, William S. and Nichols, Ralph G. *Perceptive Listening.* New York: CBS College Publishing, 1983.

Wolfram, Walter. *A Sociolinguistic Description of Detroit Negro Speech.* Washington, D.C.: Center for Applied Linguistics, 1969.

Wolvin, Andrew D. and Coakley, Carolyn Gwynn. *Listening.* Dubuque, Iowa: William C. Brown Co. Publishers, 1982.

Zimmerman, Don and West, Candace. "Sex Roles, Interruptions and Silences in Conversation." In *Language and Sex: Difference and Dominance.* Barrie Thorne and Nancy M. Henley, Eds. Rowley, Massachusetts: Newbury House, 1975.